TUTOR MANUAL

This tutorial manual is based on the Orton-Gillingham
multisensory approach for teaching persons who have
experienced difficulty in learning to read, write or spell.

By Dorothy Blosser Whitehead and
revised with Elizabeth Barton, 1993.

Dedicated to the tutors and students of:
• Language Skills Therapy
• Fundamentals of Written Language, Inc.
• Dyslexia Institute of Oregon, Inc.

Preface

This tutor manual is designed to be used by tutors learning the multisensory ORTON-GILLINGHAM method of teaching basic reading, writing and spelling skills. It is alphabetic, phonetic, systematic, sequential and cumulative and is taught directly, in a simultaneous multisensory presentation. The students use the modalities of hearing, seeing, saying and writing simultaneously.

Orton-Gillingham was designed originally in the 1920's for persons identified as having dyslexia, which can be defined as failure to master the necessary basics of one's native language despite traditional classroom teaching. It starts with a single sound with its written symbol and progresses, as fast as a student can assimilate it successfully, to words made up of known sounds, phrases, sentences, paragraphs and finally, books. Phonetic principles are taught synthetically, from parts to the whole, with syllable division, spelling rules and generalizations taught directly. Linguistic reading materials are used first as they are comprised of simple elements of our language and insure immediate success on the part of the student. The reasoning process is deductive, and nothing is assumed or left for the students to discover for themselves. Direct teaching of meaning for comprehension is taught through reading and in outlining and composition writing. Vocabulary increases slowly but surely as the tutoring progresses toward acquisition of basic language skills.

The Orton-Gillingham approach is the result of a cooperative effort by Samuel T. Orton and his wife, June, Anna Gillingham and Bessie Stillman. Orton was a neuropsychiatrist and pathologist; his wife was a psychiatric social worker. Anna Gillingham was an educator and psychologist and Bessie Stillman was a master classroom teacher. Their combined talents in many areas produced this remarkably effective method which has stood the test of time with its sound teaching practices. Many other successful methods have been based upon the principles inherent in it. Dr. Orton was also the first professional to distinguish language learning disabilities from mental defects, emotional problems, sensory deficits and brain damage.

This is not an easy method to learn to use, nor is it a rapid way to teach a person to read, write or spell. But it is a thorough way and most important of all, **it works.**

Dorothy B. Whitehead
Portland, Oregon 1993

Table of Contents

Table of Contents

APPENDIX

• Tutorial Manual Re-Order Form •

Training In Orton/Gillingham For One Academic Year

September   **First group session:** Overview of various reading programs and their difference from Orton-Gillingham. Explanation of language triangle. Introduction of sounds and practice between partners.

October   **Second group session:** More sounds practice. Discussion of the philosophy of tutoring. (Tips for Tutors)

Third group session: Lesson demonstration. Explanation of how to use the Tutor Manual.

Match tutors with students; arrange schedules. Trainers test each student to determine knowledge of sounds and their corresponding symbols. The Sound-Spelling checklist is filled out. The trainer teaches the first lesson based upon the Sound-Spelling Checklist information.

November through May   **Monthly meetings.** Various topics will be discussed:
• History of Orton-Gillingham
• Individual tutoring problems
• Observation of tutors
• Monthly reports to teachers
• Testing
• Test interpretation
• Materials review
• Medical research

Trainers will meet with individual tutors to answer questions. A tutor may ask a trainer to teach a lesson as a demonstration. After an observation, the trainer will look at the lesson plan and the student's written work to make certain that they match.

Tutors record their lesson questions and feelings on lesson plan pages or in a journal. The tutors will be expected to take notes at any lecture or seminar related to reading, writing or spelling and turn in a summary.

The practicum consists of 150 hours of one-on-one practice tutoring, of at least two students and under regular supervision by the instructors.

Two years are necessary to master this approach.

- Remember, the person you are tutoring probably has had a history of difficulty and/or academic failure in school. Because of this, during your lessons: be patient, be honest, give legitimate praise, be caring and be success-oriented for him/her.

- Use direct instruction, which means that you demonstrate anything you are introducing. Make certain that all students know what you want them to do.

- Students should have at least a 90% to 95% success rate every lesson. Tell them what you want them to know.

- If a concept is difficult for a student to remember, keep repeating it but move on slowly. (Some students may never hear the difference between short vowels /e/ and /i/.)

- Be sure to give your students six seconds think-time to answer, if needed. Many of our population need more time to respond. It may take time to assimilate what has been asked of them, as well as to retrieve it from their memory.

- All parts of the lessons must be built around the cards already mastered. All reading and writing must consist only of words made up of known sounds.

- Your students need repetition and an increasing response rate. They need to say the cards as fast as you can present them in order to put them into long-term memory. You will need to over-teach, and they will need to over-learn.

- Try to introduce something new every week and let your students check off the concepts that have been introduced. This helps them to "buy into" the slow process, as they can see their progress.

- Ask your students if they make a decoding or encoding error, "What do you hear in that word?" not "What do you see?" Remember this is primarily an auditory approach and our goal is to tie their auditory-visual-kinesthetic senses together. **Our goal is to teach them to hear what they are looking at and to spell what they hear.**

- Never permit yourself to show anger, impatience or disgust. Keep reassuring your students that with time, they will learn it.

- Discourage guessing at words. Your job is to teach them to think and to give them the tools so they do not need to guess.

- Try to keep the students from being upset when they have a bad lesson. Our population has days when the synapses seem sluggish and it is not anyone's fault. Reassure them and say, "You'll remember better next time." And they will!

- Lift the whole learning problem onto your shoulders and take the responsibility for your student's learning. Tell them you know how to help them and then proceed to show them! Say, "It's my fault you've forgotten that, because I haven't given it to you often enough. You'll get it soon."

- Remember to teach by questioning. Ask questions continually in your teaching. This is the only way you can test what you have taught.

- Emphasize the positive with statements such as, "good thinking," "excellent penmanship," etc. Build up their self-esteem by pointing out what has been learned during that lesson. Ignore mistakes and failure as much as possible.

- Be certain that your students sound out the words for themselves. Don't help them too much. They shouldn't be trying to read anything that is too difficult for them. If they make an error in the middle of a word, ask them what they <u>hear</u> in the middle of that word. If they make an error at the beginning or end, ask them what they <u>hear</u> when they look at the beginning or end of that word.

- Students should read everything they write. This way, they can learn to edit their own mistakes. (Make sure that they read exactly what they wrote, not what they intended to write.) This helps them to learn to hear what they write and eventually hear it as they write it.

- Be certain to keep the amount of teacher talk to a minimum. The ratio of student response to teacher should be 90:10.

- Multisensory teaching is Orton's rationale behind this methodology. While it has an auditory emphasis, we use all modalities in a lesson.

- Include AVK in every lesson.

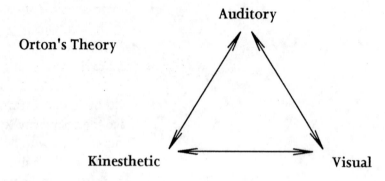

Orton's Theory

- If your student has an attention deficit and difficulty concentrating, change tasks as often as possible. It may be necessary to have 15 or 20 different tasks instead of the usual four parts to the lesson.

- Remember, be positive at all times! They need it and deserve it for they're working harder than they have ever gotten credit for in the past.

Sound-Spelling Checklist — Pronunciation Guide

m	s₁	f	b	i₁	h	j	k	p	t	c₁	o₁	r	l	n	g	ck	th₁	th₂	u₁	d	e₁
/m../	/s../	/f../	/b/	/i../	/h/	/j/	/k/	/p/	/t/	/k/	/o../	/r../	/l../	/n../	/g/	/k/	/th/ voiced	/th/ unvoiced	/u/ /ə/	/d/	/e../

ch₁	tch	sh	w	wh	y	z	x	qu	s₂	ph	Beg. con. Blends	End Blends	Spelling ll ff ss zz	a-e	e-e	i-e	o-e	u-e₁
/ch/	/ch/	/sh../		/woo/ /wh../	/y/	/z../	/ks/	/kwoo../	/z../	/f../				/ā/	/ē/	/ī/	/ō/	/yü/

u-e₂	y-e	Wild Old Words	Hard and Soft C	Hard and Soft G	ble etc.	ing etc.	dge	ed₁	ed₂	ed₃	Sight Words	Syl. Div. Rule #1	y₃	y₂	y₁	a₂	e₂	i₂	a₂
/oō/	/ī/		/k/ - /s/	/g/ - /j/			/j/	/ed/	/t/	/d/		c/c	/i/	/ē/	/ī/	/ā/	/ē/	/ī/	/ā/

Syl. Div. Rule #2	ck spell. gen.	tch Spell. Gen.	dge Spell. Gen.	Sight Words	or	ar	er	ir	ur	a₃	e₂	i₂	a₂	o₂	u₂	u₃
v̄/	ck - ke	tch - ch	dge - ge		/or/	/är/	/ər/	/ər/	/ər/	/o/ /ä/	/ē/	/ī/	/ā/	/ō/	/yü/	/oō/

a₄	aw	au	ea₁	ea₂	ea₃	ey	igh	eigh	ue₁	ue₂	ew₁	ew₂	ei₁	ei₂	ch₃	oo₂	oo₁	oy	sion₂	sion₁	tion
	/o/ /ä/														/sh/			/oi/	/zhun/	/shun/	/shun/

o - ä	o₃	u₄	ea₁	ea₂	ea₃	ey	igh	eigh	ue₁	ue₂	ew₁	ew₂	ei₁	ei₂	ch₃	oo₂	oo₁	oy	oi	ai	ay
/o/ /ä/	/ə/	/oō/	/ē/	/ē/	/ā/	/ā/ /ē/	/ī/	/ā/	/ōō/	/yü/	/yü/	/ōō/	/ē/	/ā/	/sh/	/ōō/	/ōō/	/oi/	/oi/	/ā/	/ā/

ou₁	ou₂	ch₂	oe	oa	ee	er	ar	ur	ir	ey	ie₁	ie₂	ow₁	ow₂	Silent Letters
/ou/	/ōō/	/k/	/ō/	/ō/	/ē/	/ər/	/ar/	/ər/	/ī/	/ē/	/ī/	/ē/	/ou/	/ō/	

Spelling rules / labels

Spelling Silent e · Spelling Doub. Rule · Spelling ie - ei · Spelling y Ending · Silent Letters

Ending Plurals	Possessives	Contractions	Prefixes	Suffixes	Dictionary	Accent	Homonyms	3 Syllable Irregular

Diacritical markings will vary depending upon the dictionary.

Sound-Spelling Checklist

Student Checklist

m	a₁	s₁	f	b	i₁	h	j	k	p	t	c₁	o₁	r	l	n	g	ck	th₁	th₂	u₁	d	e₁
ch₁	tch			wh	w	sh																
u-e₂		y-e			z	y	x	qu	ph	s₂					Spelling ll ff ss zz							
	Hard and Soft C		Hard and Soft G		dge	ed₁	ed₂	ed₃	y₁	y₂	y₃	a₂	e₂	i₂	o₂	u₂	u₃					
Wild Old Words	Syll. Div. Rule #2		ck Spell. Gen.	ble etc.	ing etc.	Sight Words		Beg. con. Blends	End Blends				Syl. Div. Rule #1									
											a₃	e₃	i₃	ur	ir	ar	er	or	ay	ai	tion	sion₁ sion₂	a₃	Spelling Doub. Rule	Spelling Silent e
ch₂	o₃	u₄	ea₁	ea₂	ea₃	aw	au	ou₁ on₂		tch Spell. Gen.	dge Spell. Gen.	oa	oe	ee	ai	ay	oi	oy	oo₁	oo₂	ow₁	ow₂	ie₁	ie₂
									eigh	igh	ey	ea₃	ue₁	ue₂	ew₁	ew₂	ei₁	ei₂	ch₃	Spelling y Ending	Spelling ie – ei	Silent Letters
Ending Plurals	Possessives	Contractions	Prefixes	Suffixes	Dictionary	Accent	Homonyms	3 Syllable Irregular														

a₁-/ă/
a₂-/ā/
a₃-o/ä
a₄-/ə/

s₁-/s/
s₂-/z/
c₁-/k/
c₂-/s/

o₁-/ŏ/
o₂-/ō/
o₃-/ə/
th₁-voice
th₂-unv.

u₁-/ŭ/
u₂-/yü/
u₃-/ōō/
u₄-/ōō/

ch₁-/ch/
ch₂-/k/
ch₃-/sh/
u-e₁-/yü/
u-e₂-/ōō/

ed₁-/ĕd/
ed₂-/t/
ed₃-/d/
y₁-/ī/
y₂-/ē/
y₃-/ĭ/

sion₁-/sion/
sion₁-/zhun/
oo-/ōō/
oo-/ōō/

ou₁-/ou/
ou₂-/ōō/
ea₁-/ē/
ea₂-/ĕ/
ea₃-/ā/

ow₁-/ou/
ow₂-/ō/
ie₁-/ē/
ie₂-/ī/

ei₁-/ā/
ei₂-/ē/
ue₁-/ōō/
ue₂-/yü/
ew₁-/yü/
ew₂-/ōō/

Sound Spelling Checklist Explanation

The Sound-Spelling Checklist is the foundation of this tutor notebook. It is a road map that may be followed exactly by an inexperienced tutor. While it is a random order of presentation of the sounds and concepts in the reading-spelling continuum, it has been used successfully in this order by beginning tutors. A more experienced tutor may feel free to vary the order to suit any particular student as long as the gaps are filled in and all of the concepts are covered within the capability of a given student.

After testing, the sounds that are known are checked off on the Sound-Spelling Checklist and the cards separated into two packs: the known and the unknown. A rubber band is placed around each of these and another one around both to keep the two packs together.

As a student is taught a new sound, the card is moved from the unknown pack into the known one. This is an exciting event for the student and he/she will often beg for a new card because of the pleasure of seeing the known pile grow and the unknown diminish. A great motivator is the fact that the students can be told in the beginning they are going to learn the 44 sounds of the English language. When the students have learned them all so that they are firmly fixed in their repertoire and can apply them correctly, then they will be able to decode any word in the English language, except for French words. Our language is 80% phonetic and can be "sounded out." However, most of the 20% that is unphonetic is manageable.

The student will also be taught to make educated guesses in spelling, based upon the frequency of spelling patterns. As the tutoring progresses and the Sound-Spelling Checklist fills up, the students feel more confident and hopeful that at last there is proof that they, indeed, will be able to master this difficult skill of reading, as well as its opposite, spelling and writing. While we cannot expect to train these individuals to become perfect spellers, we can teach them to become phonetic spellers so that anyone can read what they mean and direct them to the nearest dictionary, a type of hand held speller, e.g. Franklin Ace Speller, or a Spellcheck on a computer.

We are aiming for a goal of a student's feeling **in command of the print.**

Sounds Practice Sheet

Explanation:

*   The asterisk indicates a continuous sound (hold on).
     All others are stop sounds (chopped off).
/ / Encloses a sound.

Voiced	**Unvoiced**
Voiced Consonants	**Unvoiced Consonants**
* l lamp	* f fun
* m man	* s sat
* n nut	
* qu queen /kwōō.../	c cat /k/
* r rat /rer.../	h hat
* s is /z/	p pan
* v van	t top
* w wag /wōō.../	x box /ks/
* y yes /yē.../	k kite
* z zebra	
b baby	
d dog	
g go	
j jam	

Practice Phrase for Short Vowels
Ask Ed is Oz up?

Voiced Short Vowels	
* a apple	
* e Ed	
* i it	
* o ox, octopus	
* u up	

Voiced Digraphs	**Unvoiced Digraphs**
* th this	* ph phone /f/
dge hedge /j/	* sh ship
	* th thin
	* wh when
	ch chin
	tch catch /ch/
	ck duck /k/

m			
/a/ **a**			
s	**c**		
f	**ph**		
b			
/i/ **i**	**y**		
h			
j	**g**	**dge**	
k	**c**	**ck**	**ch**
p			
t	**ed**		
g			

/o/ /ä/ **o**	**a**	**au**	
aw	**ough**	**augh**	

r		
l		
n		
th		
/u/ **u**	**o**	**a**
ch	**tch**	
d	**ed**	
/e/ **e**	**ea**	

sh	**ch**	
w		
wh		
v		
y		
z	**s**	
x		
qu		
or		
ar		
er	**ir**	**ur**
oi	**oy**	
/ou/ **ou**	**ow**	
/ŏŏ/ **oo**	**u**	
/sion/ **tion**	**sion**	
/zhun/ **sion**		

/ā/ **a-e**	**a**	**ai**	**ay**	**eigh**	**ea**	**ei**	
/ē/ **e-e**	**e**	**ee**	**y**	**ey**	**ea**	**ie**	**ei**
/ī/ **i-e**	**i**	**igh**	**y**	**ie**	**y-e**		
/ō/ **o-e**	**o**	**oa**	**oe**	**ow**			
/yü/ **u-e**	**u**	**ue**	**ew**	**eu**			
/ōō/ **u-e**	**u**	**ue**	**ew**	**oo**	**ou**		

The Writing Checklist is placed with the Sound-Spelling student's checklist in every folder. This represents a record of what the student knows how to write from dictation and helps the tutor keep track of this data. During the drill part of the lesson plan, the tutor dictates sounds and the student writes the sounds. Dictation is very important as this is an <u>auditory</u> approach. **Do not omit the dictation part of a drill.**

Use the Writing Check List to teach students multiple spellings for the sounds, both consonants and vowels.

The tutor will check the sounds on the Writing Checklist as they are introduced and learned by the student. Any checked sound may be dictated if the student is able to reproduce the letter for that sound. Jump around on this task and vary the presentation, so that the student won't memorize the order. All spellings with the same sound are written horizontally. Different sounds are written vertically. Eventually a student may be expected to write all the sounds of a, e, i, o, u, etc. The multiple spellings in order of frequency, are as follows. Ususlly the frequency is not mentioned below 5th grade.

	/ā/	/ē/	/ī/	/ō/	/yü/	/o͞o/	/o/ /ä/	/ər/	/e/	/u/ /ə/	/o͝o/
SPELLING FREQUENCY	a	e	i	o	u	oo	o	er	e	u	oo
	a-e	ee	i-e	o-e	u-e	ew	au	ir	ea	a	u
	ai	ea	igh	oa	ue	u	aw	ur		o	
	ay	y	y	ow	ew	u-e	ough	or			
	eigh	e-e	ie	oe	eu	ou	augh	ar			
	ei	ie	y-e			ue		ear			
		ei									
		ey									

The student's good thinking results from a firm foundation of knowledge and the tutor's job is to provide that foundation.

Lesson Plan

There are four parts to a lesson plan.

   I. Drill (sounds and dictation)

   II. Writing (letter formation)

   III. Spelling

   IV. Reading

Lesson plans are written in a notebook and kept with the student's folder. The student's written work is dated and saved. The following is an outline of the procedure to be followed during each lesson.

I. Drill

A. Sounds.

1. Hold the Phonics Cards pack upright while resting your wrist on the table. Snap each card down as the student says the correct sound (use only cards already taught to the student.) This builds reflexes and eventually the student will respond more rapidly than you can turn the cards.

2. You may then make words with the cards which the student can sound out.

3. Spread out certain cards and ask the student to pick out the cards which spell m-a-n, etc. Be sure to sound out each word slowly.

4. Place a short vowel on the table. Then place any known consonant at the beginning and end. Continue to place new cards on top of beginning and ending consonants to make real or nonsense words. This is good decoding practice! Do not put **r**, **w**, **y**, or **qu** at the end of a word, or **c** or **g** with an **e**, **i**, or **y** after it at the beginning.

B. Drill cards for dictation. Use in conjunction with the writing check list.

1. Take up the cards individually and dictate from them. You say the sound. Have the pupil echo the sound while writing the sound one line at a time, e.g.

    b _____

    a _____

    f _____ etc.

> The most important part of the lesson is **dictation** of sounds in the drill, words, phrases and sentences.

2. Some sounds will have more than one symbol. The different symbols for the same sound will go on the same line horizontally, e.g.

b		
a		
f		
c	k	ck
m		
s		

II. Writing

Teach letter formation, italic or cursive (page 108-109) by families according to how the letters are formed.

III. Spelling

A. After you dictate a word have the student say the individual sounds aloud as he or she writes the word. /m/ - /a/ - /n/ = man

B. Phrases can be dictated using the cards known. bad man, fat man, etc.

C. Sentences will come next and, when the pupil is ready, capital letters may be added along with punctuation. Simplified capital letters may be taught if the student has difficulty with small muscle coordination in writing (dysgraphia). Have students read words, phrases and sentences aloud at the end of each lesson.

D. Spelling rules and generalizations will be taught one at a time at this point.

E. Teach syllable division.

IV. Reading

A. Reading material must be carefully picked to fit exactly with the sequence of sounds which have been taught and learned by the student.

B. All material will be read aloud. It is a good idea to alternate reading after a month or so, one sentence each, then one paragraph each and finally one page each. It helps to speed the stories along and heighten the interest of the student.

Decoding must be somewhat smooth before comprehension questions can be asked. Students must be helped to think about what they are reading while they are reading aloud but only after the decoding is smooth.

Comprehension becomes more important as the reading process advances. This is accomplished by asking questions at the end of a paragraph or story.

Never do silent reading during tutoring as this is done in the classroom.

Pacing is getting the student to do more and enjoy it more. Good pacing means increasing the intensity of the lesson and accomplishing more in less time.

TUTOR	STUDENT
I. DRILL	
A. Present drill pack, one at a time as fast as possible. Shuffle cards occasionally.	A. Student responds orally with correct sound for each card. Allow time for thinking.
B. Dictate same sounds to student.	B. Student writes sounds, one to a line, vertically.
C. Make words with drill pack, or present phonics wheel.	C. Student blends sounds together to make words. Blends words from phonics wheel.
II. WRITING (cursive)	
A. Teach roundies, **a, c, d, g, o, q.**	A. Student writes roundies separately, tracing or copying.
B. Teach upswing on **a, c, d, g, o, q.**	B. Writes upswings on **a, c, d, g, o, q.**
III. SPELLING	
A. Dictate words using known sounds.	A. Student repeats word, writes word from dictation, saying sounds aloud as he or she writes.
B. Dictate phrases using above.	B. Repeats phrases, writes phrases saying sounds aloud simultaneously.
C. Teach Spelling Rule Double ll, ff, ss, zz.	C. Practices spelling rule.
IV. READING	
A. Sit on left, point at left side of every word at first to build up left to right decoding.	A. Pupil reads back every word and phrase he has written.
B. May read alternate sentences, paragraphs or pages.	B. Reads storybook chosen to fit above lesson plan, based on known sounds only.

Phonics Cards

Here ia an example of a Phonics Card used in lesson drills. It appears as actual size.

Front

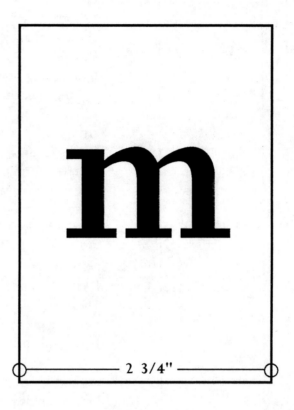

Back

FRONT   **BACK**

m	m man /m.../
a	a_1 apple /a.../
s	s_1 sat /s.../

I. Drill:
- Teach cards **m**, **a**$_1$, and **s**$_1$.
- Show card, say sound and have student point to correct card.
- Show card and have student say sound.
- Dictate sound, have student write sound, one line at a time (going down the page). Use sound/spelling writing checklist.

II. Writing:
- Work on letter formation in either italic or cursive. Cursive writing can be taught separately from the known sound cards. Use letter name. (Pg. 108-109)
- Make certain pencil grip is correct, three fingers equally balanced. See illustration below.

III. Spelling:
- Dictate: am   sam   mas
- These are called **closed syllables.** They always end in a consonant and have a short vowel.
- Have student say sounds as he/she writes.

IV. Reading:
- Blend sounds into words or nonsense syllables with the student.   /a/ - /m/
                                     /s/ - /a/ - /m/
                                     /m/ - /a/ - /s/
- Use cards to form words.
- Hold onto these and all other continuous sounds. Refer to the *Sounds Practice Sheet* on page #8.

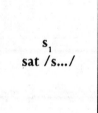

Correct Pencil Grip

Blending:
This is the most difficult task of all Make certain that all sounds with an asterisk* are prolonged (Sounds Practice Sheet pg. #8). Hang onto these and then say "Say it fast" to pull the sounds into a word. Blend the sounds with the student at first until the student can blend on his or her own.

f

f
fun /f.../

I. Drill:
- Teach **f** card when student is ready for a new sound.*
- Cards: Student says sounds of cards s, a, m, f.
- Dictate sounds. Student writes sounds one line per sound.
- * It may take a week or two before a student can handle a new card. Remember a lesson must have 95% success.

II. Writing:
- Practice letter formation.

III. Spelling:
- Dictate: am, man, Sam, mas, fam, maf, fas, faf.

IV. Reading:
- Blend sounds m, a, s, and f into real and nonsense words; by "hanging onto" the sounds and then "saying it fast."
- Have the student read what he or she has written.

---

b

b
baby /b/

I. Drill:
- Teach new sound /**b**/.
- Cards - student says sounds as cards are shown
  /**m**/, /**a**/, /**s**/, /**f**/, /**b**/.
- Dictate sounds. Student writes sounds one below the other.

II. Writing:
- Letter formation. Use letter names not sounds.
- Some students confuse **b** and **d**. If the student is right handed, teach him to make a fist in the shape of a **b** with his left hand (thumb up). If the student is left handed, teach him to make a fist in the shape of a **d** with his right hand (thumb up). The student must look at his hand before writing or reading a **b** or **d**. (Research shows that if an error is made, it takes 1,500 correct responses to correct this error permanently.)

III. Spelling:
- Dictate words made up of letters m, a, s, f, b.

| mab | ma | am | Sam | sas | sab | bab | bam |
| fab | fam | fas | saf | baf | maf | bas | |

IV. Reading:
- Read spelling words.

1 'o clock

To aid a student with **b-d letter confusion**, teach the formation of the letters differently.

A **b** is formed from the top down, line first and then the ball. A **b** is in the tall letter family of l, h, k, b, t these letters start with a straight line. The letter **d** is a roundie that begins at one o'clock and circles counter-clockwise.

Make certain that all students can tell you which is their right hand. For right-handed students, have them memorize: "I write with my right hand." This directional concept must be tied to the student's body for constant reference.

Forget the left and the letter **d**. It will fall into place after the **b** is learned. Teach one concept at a time. Never pair concepts with dyslexic students. Always teach one concept firmly. The other will fall into place. Have the student tell you the memorized phrase: "b-ball-right", making certain that he knows what he is saying in relation to the ball on the letter **b**.

As time passes, the student will then be able to think before he guesses at a **b** or a **d** in a word.

We don't need workbooks in tutoring as they are visual. Instead we bombard the auditory and kinesthetic with dictation.

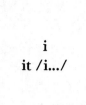

i

it /i.../

I. Drill:
• Add **i** to the m, a, s, f, and b cards.
• Cards: Student says sounds.
• Dictate sounds of cards to student. Student writes sounds.

II. Writing:
• Letter formation only.

III. Spelling:
• Compare and contrast **a** and **i** by varying the words.
  From now on, always compare and contrast short
  vowels. Dictate a list of the <u>same</u> short vowel words only if
  introducing a new card.
• Dictate words made of m, a, s, f, b, and i.

| am | Sam | sim | bas | mab | bam | saf |
| sab | mas | bab | bim | mib | mis | sif |

IV. Reading:
• Read spelling words.
• Hold onto the short vowel sound.

Small Steps

Our teaching approach is systematic and cumulative. Sometimes we need to back up on a concept. If a student has
difficulty in mastering a task, break it into the simplest
components and teach one step at a time.

Example: Teaching comparison of /**a**/ and /**i**/.

1. Student points to the **a** or **i** cards as tutor says sound
   only.
2. Student points to **a** or **i** as tutor dictates words with these
   sounds, e.g. man, pin, lab, lam, Tim, etc.
3. Student separates out and says vowel sound when tutor
   dictates words.
4. Student writes **a** or **i** when tutor dictates words.
5. Student writes whole word when tutor dictates words.

AUDITORY EXERCISES FOR SPELLING PRACTICE

The following exercises are designed for oral dictation by the tutor. The student will write the sounds the teacher asks for. It teaches the student to hear sounds in words. This is the beginning of their "phoneme segmentation".

Beginning Consonants: ————————————————
• The students will write the beginning sound, m, a, s, f, and b.

Elementary:
map, sip, mop, fat, bam, fib, bib, bop, sib, sum, mob, met, fin, bin

Advanced:
bash, fend, fell, mold, sect, fish, mind, fond, bend, send, find, sand, simp

Ending Consonants: ————————————————
• The student will write the end sound.

Elementary:
rim, nab, Sam, bum, sass, toss, him, ham, pass, blab, stuff, skiff

Advanced:
slab, staff, glum, grab, class, whim, film , dress, ebb, rub, slim

Medial Short Vowels: ————————————————
• The student will write the short vowel sound /a/ or /i/.
• Contrast a and i. This may be used as a check of weaknesses of individual students.
    apple /a/ it /i/

Elementary:
mat, bin, cap, sat, sit, lip, has, rat, sag, ram, tin, tap, tip, tad, rag, lag, lid, tan, tag, lab, hit, did, jam, Jim, bit, hat, sap, gap, rip, pin, sin

Advanced:
grab, grip, slip, simp, strap, flab, flim, drip, slim, drag, drab, dram, primp, stab, skimp, slab, string, swag, swim, smit, slit, slat, swig, strip, strap, scram, scrap, script, slash, swish, catch, snitch, latch, mitch, pitch, clan, clad, twin, grin

h

hat /h/

I. Drill:
- Teach **h** card.
- Flash cards: Student says sounds.
- Dictate: Student writes sounds.

II. Writing:
- Teach letter formation.

III. Spelling:

Score

◇

◇   ◇

◇

Home Plate

- Introduce baseball game **S.O.S.**
  (*Gillingham's Simultaneous Oral Spelling.*)
  The rules of play are as follows:
  1. Student starts with pencil on home plate.
  2. Tutor says word.
  3. Student repeats word. (Move to 1st base.)
  4. Student identifies vowel by sound. (Move to 2nd base.)
  5. Student spells word aloud. (Move to 3rd base.)
  6. Student writes words and says letter sounds aloud as
     he or she writes. Older students may say letter names.
     (Go to home base and mark a score.)
- Dictate: am, Sam, ham, him, sim, mif, baf, sib, fas, hab.

IV. Reading:
- Have the student read what he or she has written.

S I G H T   W O R D S

Sight words are to be memorized.
Students should know them by
sight and be able to spell them.
As sight words are intoduced, put
them onto cards for memorization. Make a separate sight word
pack. **has** and **is** are sight words
at this point and may be spelled
by the tutor.

j

jam / j /

I. Drill: Teach **j** card. See-say, hear-write cards.

II. Writing: Teach letter formation (pg. 108-109).

III. Spelling: S.O.S. spelling.

IV. Reading: Student reads what he or she has written.

Words for Dictation:
jam   jas   Jim   him   bam   jab   ham   jis   his

Sentences for Dictation:
Jim <u>has</u> ham.   Jim <u>has</u> jam.   Jim jabs Sam.

NOTE:
Hereafter, follow the lesson plan format with its four parts. Only words, phrases, and sentences will be given in detail. Follow the order presented on the *Sound Spelling Checklist* and the *Writing/Spelling Checklist*

k

kite /k/

Drill • Writing • Spelling • Reading

Words for Dictation:
kam   jas   bam   hab   him   Kim
jam   <u>has</u>   mab   has   kib   kab

Sentences for Dictation:
Kim <u>has</u> jam.

p

pan /p/

Drill • Writing • Spelling • Reading

Words for Dictation:
pam   ham   hip   bap   bip   hap
him   pim   pab   jip   kas
pom

Phrases for Dictation:
Pam <u>has</u> ham.
Jim <u>is</u> a man.

t

top /t/

Drill • Writing • Spelling • Reading

Words for Dictation:
tap   tip   Tam   tat   pit
pat   pim   mat   kaf

Sentences for Dictation:
Tam hit Tim.
Tam bit Pat.
Pat sat.

Phonics Wheel

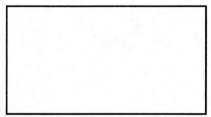

1. Begin with poster board or similar heavy material.

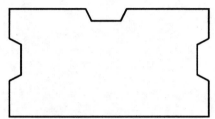

2. Following the template in the appendix cut two pieces as shown above.

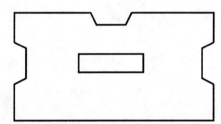

3. Cut out the window in one piece only. This will be the **front** piece. The other remaining the same will be the **back**.

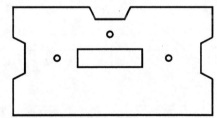

4. Place **front** on **back** and, punch holes for brads. Cut out the wheels following the template in the appendix.

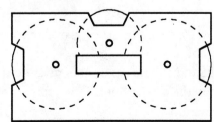

5. Sandwich wheels between the back and front. Middle wheel must be placed in back. Secure all pieces together with brads. Carefully rotate wheels and ink in the letters following the lists at the right. If letters run out they may be repeated.

The **Phonics Wheel** is used to create a variety of real and nonsense words. It is an invaluable tool used in lesson drills to teach blending. There are four phonics wheels. Phonics Wheel #1 has a closed syllable with one beginning and one ending consonant and a short vowel in the middle (cvc). Phonics Wheel #2 has a closed syllable with the digraphs added. Phonics Wheel #3 has beginning consonant blends (ccvc). Phonics Wheel #4 has beginning and ending consonant blends (ccvcc).

At the left are step by step instructions for making your own Phonics Wheel. You will find actual size templates on pages 115 and 117 of the appendix. Tear these out (or use photocopies) to pattern your cuts. Listed below are the letter patterns to be written on the wheels **after** you have finished putting your Phonics Wheel together.

Beginning Wheel				Middle	Ending Wheel			
#1	**#2**	**#3**	**#4**		**#1**	**#2**	**#3**	**#4**
b	b	bl	bl	a	b	b	b	ck
f	ch	br	br	e	ck	ck	ck	ch
g	f	cl	cl	i	d	d	d	ct
h	g	ch	ch	o	f	f	f	ft
j	h	cr	cr	u	g	ff	ff	lf
d	j	dr	dr		l	g	g	lp
l	d	fl	fl	(all	m	l	l	mp
m	l	fr	gl	short	n	ll	ll	nch
n	m	gl	gr	vowel	p	m	m	nd
p	n	gr	ph	sounds)	s	n	n	ng
r	p	ph	pl		t	p	p	nk
s	r	pl	pr		x	s	s	nt
t	sh	pr	qu		z	ss	ss	sk
v	th	qu	sc			t	t	st
w	v	sc	shr			x	x	xt
y	w	sk	sk			z	z	sh
	wh	sh	sh				zz	tch
	y	sl	sl					th
	z	sn	sn					ph
		sp	sp					rt
		st	scr					
		sw	spl					
		th	spr					
		tr	str					
		tw	th					
		wh	thr					
			tr					
			tw					
			wh					

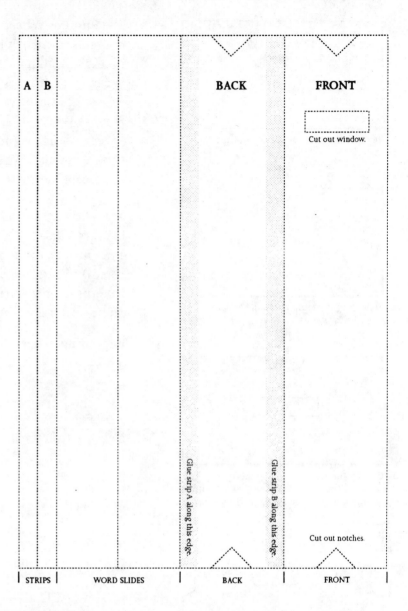

BACK

FRONT

Cut out window.

Glue strip A along this edge.

Glue strip B along this edge.

Cut out notches.

STRIPS   WORD SLIDES   BACK   FRONT

Instructions: _____

Follow these instructions to make your own tachistoscope. Use the template found on page 119 of the appendix. The template may be torn out or you may choose to use a photocopy.

1. Adhere the template to a larger piece of posterboard by running tape across the top and bottom.
2. Using an X-acto or matt knife and a metal straight edge cut out the individual pieces following the dotted lines. Don't forget to cut out the notches and the window.
3. Glue strips **A** and **B** along the edges of the back piece.
4. Apply glue to the tops of A and B and place the front on top.
5. After the glue has had sufficient time to dry insert the strips.
6. Through the window write words onto the strips.

C

c_1
cat /k/

SIGHT WORDS
<u>a</u>   <u>of</u>   <u>the</u>

Spelling:
Words are grouped randomly so the student learns to listen for differences.

Words for Dictation:

cat	Pam	Tim	Pat	pit	cam	jam	tam
bam	cab	Jim	him	Sam	bim	sip	hic
sit	cap	caf	fib	hit	kit	tap	tab
sat	ham	hat	fit	fat	hip		

Phrases for Dictation:

tit tat
fat cat
bat cap
ham fat

Sentences for Dictation:

Sam <u>has a</u> cab.
Tam <u>is</u> fat.
Pat hit Tim.
Sam bit Jim.
Pam <u>has</u> fat ham.

> **Note:**
> Tell the student that no one can tell the **c** from a **k** by its sound, and that you will tell them which to use.

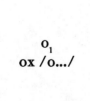

o_1
ox /o.../

Rule:
Hold onto short vowel sound, /o.../.

Words for Dictation:

job	sob	pot	Tom	cof	cob	Bob	hot
pop	fob	fom	bom	sot	top	sop	mom
cop	hop	mob	pip				

Phrases for Dictation:
pop top
hip hop
hot pot
top hat

Sentences for Dictation:
Bob <u>is</u> hot.
Mom sobs.
Tom <u>is a</u> cop.
<u>The</u> top <u>of</u> <u>the</u> pot <u>is</u> hot.

> **Tutors:** Classroom work is not your job. Your job is to help the student get a foundation so he or she can function in the classroom.

AUDITORY EXERCISES FOR SPELLING PRACTICE

The student will **write only the short vowel /o/, added to** /a/ and /i/.

Elementary:

bot, cot, cat, sit, sack, rot, rit, lit, lob, lot, lib, lag, log, lam, lim, lom, fat, fit, lop, lap, cat, lip, rid, rig, rag, rod, lab, ram, rim, pom, pin, pan, fan, Dan, ran, can, sin, sip, sap, sop, lop, ant, in, on, an, gin, Don, Ron, pon, von, con, cop, sop, fop, tin, tan, tip, till, tap, top, hop, hip, hat, flip, flap, slap, clap, clip, clop, grip, grap, slit, slot, slat, flat, flit, frill

Advanced:

swam, swig, rift, raft, slop, simp, slag, whisk, frock, whish, whist, waft, shim, which, split, splash, pinch, plank, plots, plop, split, splat, splotch, scratch, fringe, champ, pinch, chink, shank, shock, blotch, shisk, rasp, chit, brash, slosh, slash, pitch, patch, botch, ratch, rash, risk, stash, skit, crisp, crash, clasp, clip, slop, clap, cramp, crimp, slant, stint, stand, stance, strand, sting, long, fringe, hinge, binge, badge, slash, frisk, brisk, frost, link, lank

"Our purpose is to get the student to an independent level. We have only a short time."
D.B.W.

"For wisdom is to know how little one knows. Teaching at its best, best communicates both charity and humanity."
Elizabeth Drews
"Learning Together", 1972
Prentice Hall

r

r
rat /rer.../

Rule:
r is a very difficult sound to teach. Hold onto it, /rer.../.

Words for Dictation:

Ron	rab	ram	rob	rot	rat	rib	Rob
rap	rim	rip	ras	raf	rop	rif	rom

Phrases for Dictation:
fat rat
rip-rap
on the map

Sentences for Dictation:
Ron is tops.
Rob has a fat rib.
His bag has a big rip.
The rat bit Rob.
Ron hit his hip.
Jog on the mat.

S I G H T   W O R D S
his

l

l
lamp /l.../

Rule:
Hold onto l, /l.../.

Words for Dictation:

Lil	lop	lam	lap	lip	rip	ril	lim
lab	rol	cal	cam	jol	jal	Hal	hil
Bill	fal	fol	col	sil	Sal	mam	pal

Phrases for Dictation:
fat cat
fat lip
at the lab

Sentences for Dictation:
Hal has a fat lip.
Cal bit his lip.
Lil is hip.
A big cat is on his lap.
Sal is a pal.
Lil has a nap

The fat rat sat on the cat.

n
n
nut /n.../

Rule:
Hold onto sound, /n.../.

Words for Dictation:

nag	ran	ban	lan	nam	nob	Lon	Ron
san	nab	man	pan	tin	can	con	not
non	bin	han	Jan	pin	rin	fan	Nan

Phrases for Dictation:
tin pan
sad man
tin man

Sentences for Dictation:

Tim can sit.	The bad rat ran.
Tim is a man.	Jan can pin Nan.
Mom is not mad.	Jan is a ham.
Pam has a nap.	Ron can nab Rob.

g
g
go /g/

Words for Dictation:

big	bag	gap	gab	pig	jog	gal	fog
tag	sag	rig	big	bog	lag	got	fig
mag	rag	gag	gob	log	jig	hag	hog
tog	nag	cog	nog	lag			

Phrases for Dictation: **Sentences for Dictation:**

Phrases for Dictation:	Sentences for Dictation:
big hog	A big gob of figs.
rag bag	Gas the rig.
big bag	Tag the bag.
big pig	Fog in the bog.

Reading: The student must always read aloud what he has written during the spelling section. At this level the following phonetic books are recommended:
- Bloomfield, Let's Read Book
- Teaching Box Books 1. Sam 2. Nan 3. Nat
- Primary Phonics, Mac & Tab
- Stories for Sounds, Level A
- Modern Curriculum Press: Max, Sam & Al

ck
duck /k/

Note:
ck may be taught as a sound only. Dictate for spelling only if the student can handle it.

Rule:
ck comes after a short vowel in one syllable words. For older students you can teach that we use a **ck** after a short vowel in short words (see page 53).

Words for Dictation:

lack	sock	pick	rock	Jack	rack	Mick	rack
jock	Rick	hick	mock	Sack	back	hock	Mack
lock	pack	hack	hick	sick	lick	pock	Nick

Sentences for Dictation:

Sit on a tack.	Pick a big sock.
Rig the nag to the rock.	Jack has a back pack.
Mack is a hick.	Lock the rig to the rock.
Pick the lock.	Pack the bag, Jack.
Rick jogs.	Rock the rig, Mick.

• Student reads sentences aloud after writing them.

S I G H T	W O R D S
to	put

th₁ this
/ t h / voiced
th₂ thin
/ t h / unvoiced

th has two sounds.

th₁ Voiced as in this and the.
th₂ Unvoiced as in thin and think.

Words for Dictation:

this	path	math	hath	thin	them	that	bath
path	gath	than	the	thus	thick		

Sentences for Dictation:

This bath is hot.	The moth is in the fog.
The thin man is tan.	This thin nag is sick.
This is a big bath.	Put the moth on the rock.
That fog is thick.	

• Student reads sentences aloud after writing them.

S I G H T	W O R D S
they	there

u

u₁
up /u.../

Rule:
Hold onto sound, /u.../.

Drill:
Teach short vowel sound of **u** and add to drill pack.

Writing:
Continue and review letter formation.

Words for Dictation:

mug	gun	sum	run	bus	lug
fun	cut	run	sub	tuck	pub
suck	pup	rub	tub	luck	gum
cub	thug	gut	pun	hug	rug
tug	nut	hut	luck	muck	duck

Phrases and Sentences for Dictation:

hot tub	bad luck
Rub the cub.	Run, Ron!
Hug the pup.	Put the duck on the rug.
This is a hot dog in a bun.	The thug hit Mick.
That is a bug on a rug.	Mack cut a rug.

• Student reads sentences aloud after writing them.

Rub the cub.

AUDITORY EXERCISES FOR SPELLING PRACTICE

Add /**u**/ to /a/, /i/ and /o/.
Have the student write the short vowel sounds **a, i, o,** or **u,** only.

Elementary:
hug, rug, doll, rag, bog, sill, pat, tip, pit, sip, lip, lop, lam, man, min, sin, rot, not, nap, nip, kit, cap, sap, lap, rip, pip, Pam, Dan, man, can, sin, fun, fit, fat, pot, pit, puff, silt, doll, pant, fill, cull, rill, ruff

Intermediate:
hung, rung, lung, sang, sing, song, sung, sunk, hank, thank, rink, cong, gong, grunge, strand, scrunch, scratch, pump, sump, gland, glint, glump, clamp, sloth, cloth, clutch, klatch, slump, gimp, grump, stretch, plunge, crumb, slant, plump

d
dog /d/

Rule:

d is presented at the end of the consonants to separate it from b. Teach letter formation. **d** begins with round part at 1 o'clock (refer to *b and d confusion on page 18.*)

Words for Dictation:

mad	dam	duck	Dan	sad	dab	had	tub
dim	Dad	tad	dug	dog	rad	bid	sub
and	Sid	dig	lid	lad	Thad	bad	lad
dock	Don	gad	God	rid	Kid	mid	
cad	pad	dub	mud	bud	dud	rug	

Phrases and Sentences for Dictation:

rug pad	Don had a duck.
rad Thad	The dog dug in the mud.
rag bag	Dig in the mud.
mad dog	The man had a rag bag.
Dot ran on the dam.	The lad <u>was</u> sad.
A mad rat ran on the rug.	The lad hid in the tub.
The sub <u>was</u> at the dock.	The dog hid in the rug.

S I G H T   W O R D S

<u>was</u>

e₁
Ed /e.../

Rule:

Short **e** is the last and most difficult vowel to teach. It is often confused with short i. It takes a lot of practice. Remember to hold onto the sound.

Words for Dictation:

Ed	peck	Meg	fed	red	led	beg
red	hem	leg	Len	met	set	men
Ken	let	met	ten	get	den	bet
hen	pen	Jeb	Ben	leg	Peg	net
beck	deck	peg	pet	sled	rest	

Phrases and Sentences for Dictation:

The hen did peck Ed.	Let them run neck and neck.
Get a net and set it up.	Beth and Seth had a hen.
Let the pet run.	Beg Peg to let Len pet the hen.
Set the pet on the bed.	Ben and the men led the pack.
Set up the net.	Jeb led Peg to the deck.

- A sentence to practice all the short vowels: **Ask Ed is Oz up.** Put on a card and place in front of student for constant reference. Many thanks to Alice Koontz for this sentence.

Beg Peg to let Len pet the hen.

"If they know it but can't use it, they don't know it."
D.B.W.

AUDITORY EXERCISES FOR SPELLING PRACTICE

Add /**e**/ to /a/, /i/, /o/, and /u/. The student will write the short vowel /a/, /o/, /i/, and /u/, or /e/ only.

Elementary and Intermediate:
bag, beg, big, bog, buf, rum, rat, rit, wet, sot, fen, wint, send, hint, hand, hip, stunt, fuss, when, which, lot, lump, lent, lint, tent, spent, shunt, send, mist, mast, shed, slid, slump, slant, sled, red, pram, primp, blest, pent, bunt, scant, shred, mist, lest, list, test, pent, pant, punt, rest, just, bust, best, pest, wrest, crash, crest, slash, swish, yelp, gulp, kelp, bulb, gulf, self, twig, elm, lilt, pend, wend, hint, stint, vend

ch₁
chin /ch/

tch
match /ch/

Rule:
ch starts words. **tch** ends words - after a short vowel.
Exceptions: such, much, rich, which and sandwich.
At this point, teach tch for reading purposes only.
Advanced students can handle tch for dictation also,
see *tch Spelling Generalization*, page 74.

Words for Dictation or Reading:

chin	chap	chop	chum	chip
chump	chug	ditch	Mitch	hitch
pitch	patch	chock	Chet	chick
chog	fetch	batch	match	Dutch
hutch	rich	which	such	much
check	chuck	chill	chimp	chant
pinch	bunch	chest	bench	pitch
lunch	notch	quench	crunch	trench
flinch	branch	ranch	scratch	
clutch	sketch	stitch	French	

Phrases and Sentences for Dictation or Reading:

chit chat	Fetch the batch, Mitch.
Dutch hutch	Ditch the witch.
such luck	Patch the latch, Chad.
Chad and Mitch are chums.	Pinch the chimp on the chin.
Hatch the plan, Chet.	

sh
ship /sh.../

Rule:
Hold onto sound, /**sh...**/.
sh occurs at the beginning or the end of words.

Words for Dictation:

ship	sham	shad	shall	shot	mash
lash	cash	fish	rash	dish	dash
gosh	mash	shop	shed	bash	gash
shut	hash	sash	shin	mesh	lash
mush	lush	shad	shop	shift	shaft
shack	rush	sham	crush	slush	flush
splash	flash	thrush	shunt	shaft	fresh

SIGHT WORDS

want   where   what   who

Phrases and Sentences for Dictation:

fish dish	Mash the mush.
a red sash	A shad is a fish.
lush bash	A shop is in the shed.
Shut the shop.	

w
wag /woo.../

Words for Dictation:

wet	wig	win	wit	wok	web
wag	wog	wop	wed	wob	will
wish	wept	with	witch	wind	west

Phrases and Sentences for Dictation:

wig-wag	The witch wept.
wet web	The dog will wag.
wet wig	The wok is hot.
west wind	The wick is wet.

wh
when /wh/
(unvoiced)

Words for Dictation:

whip	wham	whack	whelp	whit
when	whim	whist	whig	why

Sentences for Dictation:

Whack the whip.	Where did Same go?
When did he win?	When did he win?
What did he want?	Who shut Sam in the pen?

v
v
van /v.../

Words for Dictation:

van	ven	vip	vim	vast	vest
vet	vex	vox	viv	vent	vick
vig	vel	vec	vol	vat	

Phrases and Sentences For Dictation:

wet vest   The vet has a van.

y
y
yes /yē.../

Words for Dictation:

yes	yam	yet	yon
yen	yak	yep	yum

Phrases for Dictation:

yip yap   yen for yams

z
z
zebra /z.../

Words for Dictation:

zip zap Boz zig Oz zit zag Liz
zig-zag

Sentences for Dictation:

Roz has a zit.	Boz has zest.
Oz has zip.	Stop the zig-zag.
Zap Liz.	

x
x
box /ks/

Words for Dictation:

wax	mox	mix	box	Max	ax
six	fix	fax	lax	fox	lox
lux	sex	tax	wax	sax	flax

Phrases and Sentences for Dictation:

tax man	Fix the box.	Wax the ax.
six bits	Max the lax.	Six in a mix.

qu
**qu
queen
/kw$\overline{oo}$../**

Words for Dictation:

quiz	squid	queen	quench
quid	quip	quest	quilt
Quin	quit	quint	quick

s
**s₁
sat /s.../
s₂
is /z.../**

Rule:
- When **s** says /**z**/ it is never doubled.

Words for Dictation:

was	is	as	his

Advanced: _____

Music	miser	easel	chosen	roses	nose

ph
**ph
phone /f.../**

Note:
Dictate only if the student is capable of it.

Words for Dictation:

photo	phono	phase	Philip	phrase
phone	elephant	graph	telephone	Joseph

S I G H T   W O R D S

See page 59 for additional sight words. Add them slowly, by sight and writing.

*"Teach them to hear the words they're looking at
and to spell what they hear."*
D.B.W.

Philip is an elephant.

Drill:

Dictate the following sentences. This is an opportunity to test for all the alphabet, short vowels and digraphs. Are they **hearing** the sounds you're dictating?

Note:

For students who have not had ck, ll, ff, ss, or zz, tell them the spelling.

"Students are always letting you know where they are by their errors."
D.B.W.

1. Fat Sam sat on a mat.
2. Bat the mat.
3. Nab the bad man.
4. Pat sat on Tab's lap.
5. Pat has a fat rag bag.
6. Pam is Tim's pal.
7. The ant sat on the tan mat.
8. Nan has jam and ham.
9. Tab has a fat tan rat.
10. The ram jabs at Hal.
11. The tax man has zip.
12. Pat is a pal.
13. Sam has a bat.
14. Dad ran to the cab.
15. Hal had a cat nap.
16. I am mad at the cat.
17. The lad can pack the fat ham in the sack.
18. Jan has a cat and a pal.
19. The lad can tag the gal.
20. Tab, the lad, ran to Dad.
21. Jack can pass the quiz.
22. Ann has a bag and a sack.
23. Dad can pack the rack.
24. Jack is back.
25. Jim has a back pack.
26. Hal and Pam ran back.
27. The tan rack can sag.
28. Dick will dig in the bin.
29. Tack it in the back.
30. Tab can quack in the back.
31. The yam is in the vat.
32. Max will wax the cab.
33. The six pigs are sick.
34. The duck quacks in the back of the van.
35. The man had a pick of the cats.
36. Kill the bad rat, Jim.
37. Dad has a kiss for Mom.
38. The jam is a red gob on the rug.
39. Set the hot pot on the log.
40. The red van is in a fix.
41. The men got a tin can for the yams.
42. Set the big wet bass in a pot.
43. Shut the shed.
44. When did he lend the sled to Chad?
45. That is a thrill.
46. Thump went the chimp.
47. Ralph sits on the box.
48. The fish has a fin.
49. Sam sat with his mom.
50. That chap has a wish.
51. His chin is thin.
52. This is a hot bath.
53. The ship is at the dock.

A syllable is a word or part of a word always with a vowel sound. Nonsense syllables can occur in words but do not have meaning by themselves.

Nonsense words test student's auditory discrimination. They are particularly necessary for adults and are a true test of their application of phonics.

Phonemic awareness is what has been lacking for adult dyslexics. Auditory training using nonsense words and sentences helps strengthen this weakness.

All the syllables on this page are closed syllables. A closed syllable ends with a short vowel.

For Dictation and Reading:

das	biv	sug	glusp	plab	trint
tet	sin	quin	glub	smath	slib
pam	sal	kel	gren	twelp	blint
dus	len	plent	blump	brosk	strup
fis	geg	valp	pask	presk	strunt
hep	nov	stremp	gunt	brug	blont
rus	ros	des	slasp	slint	resk
pud	rel	vix	gop	dit	slist
sud	zon	gat	plov	ploft	grum
nup	jus	dys	smelp	drand	dant
quiv	blem	bak	nect	brint	strend
dem	plit	daf	prol	dren	blim
min	snelt	quib	shump	vok	zelp
bix	fas	fif	tob	slit	munt
dib	dis	vap	twilp	trag	yat
hom	hos	wob	nosp	rosk	blen
beb	jal	sep	sprit	glun	swust
gog	rom	jit	ven	stant	milb
plov	hab	siz	stremp	jund	sloft
wheb	peb	med	spem	plint	sproft
ron	ped	nym	bish	blip	stin
rol	sym	lis	jat	chig	strig
dos	wiz	vit	chilt	gramp	fol
lig	yid	phim	nob	kem	plet
lav	pis	mun	mep	bez	muz

Drill:
Test these blends by dictation. Say words and have the student write the beginning blends. Work into spelling whole words. Do not put these on cards. For reading use **Phonics Wheel #3.**

b l	blab	bled	blob	blot		
b r	brad	brag	bran	brat	brig	brim
c l	clad	clam	clan	clap	clip	clod	club
c r	crab	crag	cram	crib	crop		
d r	drab	drag	drip	drop	drub	drug	drum
f l	flag	flap	flat	fled	flip	flit	flop
g l	glad	glib	glum	glut		
g r	grab	gram	grid	grim	grin	grip	grit
	grog	grub				
p l	plan	plot	plug	plum	plus	
p r	pram	prig	prim	prod	prom	prop
s c	scab	scan	scat	Scot	scum	
s k	skid	skim	skin	skip	skit	
s l	slab	slag	slam	slap	slat	sled	slid
	slim	slip	slit	slob	slop	slot	slug
s n	snag	snap	snip	snub	snug	
s p	span	spat	sped	spin	spit	
s c r	scram	scrap	scrip	scrub	scrimp	
s p l	split	splat	splash			
s t r	strap	strip	strop	strum	strut	
t h r	thrush	thrift	thrill	throb		
t r	tram	trap	trim	trip	trod	trot
t w	twig	twin	twit			

Phrases and Sentences for Dictation: Appear on page #40.

"Only you, the tutor, can decide how fast to go. Use 90% to 95% success as the gauge."
D.B.W.

Ending Consonant Blends

Drill:
Test these blends by dictation. Say words and have the student write the last sounds he or she hears. Do not put these on cards. **Phonics Wheel #4** may be used for reading.

c t	act	fact	pact	tact	sect	duct
	insect					
f t	deft	left	gift	lift	rift	sift
	tuft					
l d	held	weld	meld	gild	wild	
l f	self	elf	itself	himself	gulf	
l p	gulp	pulp				
l k	bulk	hulk	sulk	bilk	silk	ilk
	milk	elk				
l t	belt	felt	melt	pelt	welt	gilt
	hilt	jilt	kilt	lilt	silt	tilt
l m	elm	film	helm			
m p	bump	dump	hump	jump	pump	romp
	imp	limp	camp	damp	lamp	vamp
	ramp	tamp	hemp			
n c h	inch	pinch	cinch	munch	hunch	lunch
n d	and	band	hand	land	sand	end
	bend	lend	rend	mend	tend	pend
	wend	bond	fond	pond	fund	wind
n t	ant	pant	rant	font	dint	hint
	lint	mint	tint	dent	lent	pent
	tent	rent	sent	vent	bunt	runt
	hunt	Lent	punt			
r t	dirt	flirt				
s k	dusk	husk	musk	rusk	tusk	desk
	disk	risk				
s t	best	jest	lest	nest	pest	rest
	test	vest	west	zest	bust	dust
	gust	just	must	rust	fist	list
x t	next					

Phrases and Sentences for Dictation: Appear on next page.

"Go as fast as you can but as slow as you must."
Anna Gillingham

Beginning Consonant Blends

Nonsense Words for Dictation:

twix   strug   slep   scrim   plim   scrip   skem   skud

Phrases for Dictation:

flip flop   drip drop   split strip   clip-clop

Sentences for Dictation:

Skip the skit.   Trot to the tram.
Snip the twig.   The cab fled.
Slap the slob.   The truck was red and black.
Scrub the skin.   Sam skids and skips.
Trim the flag.   Jan claps and grins.
Strum the drum.
The brat was in the crib.
Snip and Snap are snug in the rug.
The plan was to grab the twin flags and run.
The Scot was clad in a drab frock.

Ending Consonant Blends

Phrases for Dictation:

camp tent   a gulp of milk   the best lunch

Sentences for Dictation:

We set up the tent in camp.   Jump in the damp pond.
Cinch that winch an inch.   The husk is hemp.
The elk left the hunt.   An ant has a nest by the pond.
The elk was a hulk.   Jim held the stack on the shelf.
The tent felt damp.   He was fond of the jazz band.
Must the belt rust?   Sift the sand at the dump.
She held the lamp.   The land had a ramp to the camp.
The frog sat in the pond.
Jack left a plug of hemp in the vent.
Sam jumps and romps in the gusts of wind.
A rat did risk a trip with the cat.

Beginning and Ending Consonant Blends

Phonics Wheel #4
For Auditory Exercises, Dictation and Reading:

blend   grind   trend   plank   blind   grant   stamp
plump   draft   gland   splash   trump   plant   drift

Rule:
Double /**l**/, /**f**/, /**s**/, and /**z**/ in most one-syllable words after a short vowel.

- Tell the student when he or she hears a /s/, /f/, /l/ or /z/ at the end of a little word, the letter is doubled.
- A sentence to use as a memory device is: **Buzz off Miss Pill.**

Note:
Final s saying /z/ is never doubled; as, is, has, was, his.

Word list for spelling:

bell	ill	doll	cull	bull
dell	bill	loll	dull	full
fell	dill	Moll	gull	pull
hell	fill		hull	
jell	hill		lull	
sell	kill		mull	
tell	mill		null	
well	pill			
yell	sill			
Nell	chill			

bass	Bess	kiss	boss	cuss
lass	mess	miss	loss	muss
mass	Tess	hiss	Ross	fuss
pass	dress		toss	Guss
sass	address		cross	
brass	less		moss	
glass				
grass				
class				

gaff	Jeff	miff	off	buff
staff		tiff	doff	cuff
		cliff		duff
		sniff		guff
				huff
				muff
buzz				puff
fuzz				stuff
fizz				fluff
jazz				ruff

Sentences for Dictation:

Dan had a pill.
Her dress is a mess.
Get a whiff of that smell!
Drill for a well.
Spill the swill, Jill.
Gulls skim the waves.
Bess has a big bass.
Nell will miss the class.
Pass the stuff to Bill.
The pop in the glass will fizz.
Bill will spill the glass.
Jill fell on the hill.
I fell off the cliff.
A dog will sniff.
The class bell rings.
Jeff will pass Buzz.
Ross was cross with the class.
Smash the glass in the grass.
Jill will fill the bill.
Jan can miss the jazz drill.
Fill the glass with milk.
The lass is ill.
Did she sniff the smog?
Ross will pass Will on the hill.
Bill ran up the hill to pass the truck.
Will can till the hill.
The grass is wet from the pond.

Sentences using all the concepts taught so far:

• Short vowels, digraphs, and alphabet
• Beginning consonant blends
• Ending consonant blends
• Spelling ll, ff, ss, zz

Pass the glass, Jill.
Zip the back pack, Jeff.
Fix the six hens in the van.
Set the lid on the rim of the pan.
Fit the jam and ham in the pot.
The whip is as thin as an inch.
Fill the brass drum with grass.
The twin can grip the black twig.
Zack can chop the log.
Helen set the chips on a brick.
Did Gramps toss his hat on the bed?
A flock of hens can get stuck in the mud.
Tom will check the crack in the ship.
The men will drill on the top of the hill in the grass.
The crab will grip the frog and the shrimp in the pond.
The lad will wish for cash.
She thinks the chap is swell.
The rich man thanks his boss.
The chap has a chill.
The staff is in shock.
The winch will pinch the log.
Brush the plush shag rug.
The thrush sat in the shrub.
Brush the stuff off the step.
Crash went the trash into the bin.
Which squash was an inch thick?

Pet the dog, Zack.

"Don't assume anything! Tell the students what you want them to know - direct instruction not the discovery method."
D.B.W.

a-e

safe /ā/

e-e

these /ē/

i-e

pine /ī/

o-e

home /ō/

u-e

u-e₁
mule /ū/
u-e₂
rule /o͞o/

- **Silent e** syllables follow the pattern: vowel-consonant-silent e (v̄cȩ). The e at the end is silent and makes the preceding vowel long.
- Use silent **e** cards as a group first, shuffle them into the pack.
- "Magic e" makes the preceding vowel say its own name. Teach the student that the letters on the card represent "vowel-consonant-magic e." Teach a closed syllable, short vowel word such as rat, then add silent e to form rate. Continue this process with the word lists for dictation.
- Note that u-e has two sounds.

at - ate	mad - made	
mat - mate	rob - robe	
hat - hate	mop - mope	Detached silent e
pin - pine	plan - plane	syllables.
din - dine	rod - rode	
cot - cote	hid - hide	ete ize
rot - rote	kit - kite	ile ule
tub - tube	rip - ripe	ope eme
cub - cube	fad - fade	ene ite
cap - cape	cut - cute	ume ute

Additional materials for this level:

- Ed. Pub. Service, *Primary Phonics*
    Mac is Safe
    The Big Game
    The Joke
- Ed. Pub. Service, *More Primary Phonics*
    Babe, The Big Hit
    Make The Bed
    Mole
    A Ride on a Bus

* y-e
Teach **y-e** to students above 3rd grade only.
type   style

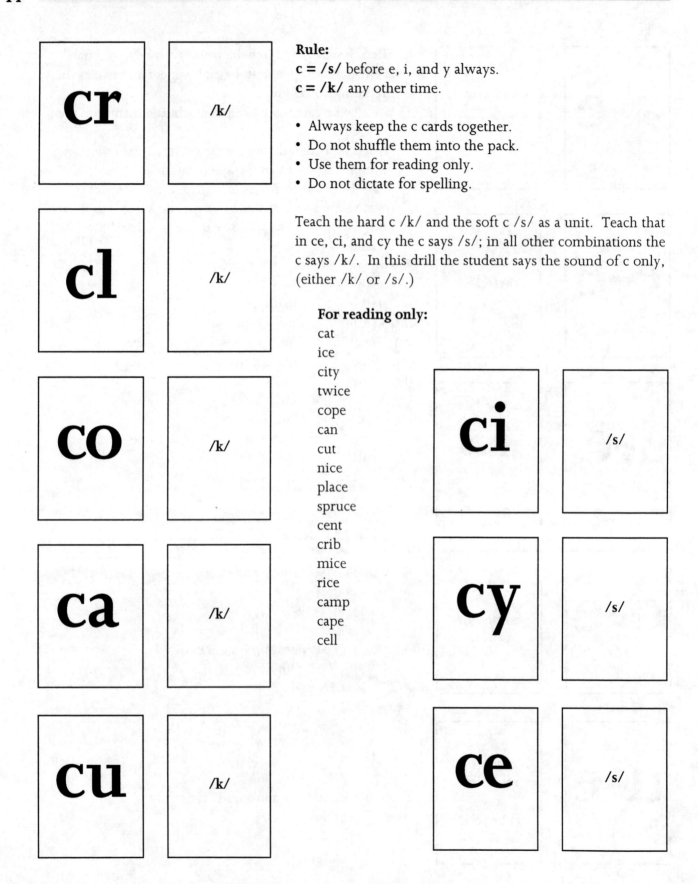

cr /k/

cl /k/

co /k/

ca /k/

cu /k/

ci /s/

cy /s/

ce /s/

Rule:
c = /**s**/ before e, i, and y always.
c = /**k**/ any other time.

• Always keep the c cards together.
• Do not shuffle them into the pack.
• Use them for reading only.
• Do not dictate for spelling.

Teach the hard c /k/ and the soft c /s/ as a unit. Teach that in ce, ci, and cy the c says /s/; in all other combinations the c says /k/. In this drill the student says the sound of c only, (either /k/ or /s/.)

For reading only:
cat
ice
city
twice
cope
can
cut
nice
place
spruce
cent
crib
mice
rice
camp
cape
cell

gu

/g/

go

/g/

ga

/g/

gr

/g/

gl

/g/

g = /g/   **dge = /j/**

g = /j/ before e, i, and y, usually
Exceptions: get, gift, girl, give, begin.

- Keep cards together.
- Do not shuffle them into the pack.
- Use them for reading only.
- Do not dictate for spelling.
- Introduce **dge** for reading only.
- For spelling generalization see pg. 75.

For Reading Only:

wage
cage
stage
age
gem
strange
singe
fringe
page
badge
ledge
bridge
dodge
budge
smudge
ridge
judge
fledge

For older students:
age /ij/ as in:
bandage
package
manage
damage
savage
voltage
village
message

ge

/j/

gi

/j/

gy

/j/

dge

/j/

ed

ed₁
rented /əd/
ed₂
jumped /t/
ed₃
sailed /d/

ed₁   ed₂   ed₃

Rule:
ed = /əd/₁ /t/₂ /d/₃

• Teach the students the following sentence as a memory device: He rent__ed__ a boat, jump__ed__ in and sail__ed__ off.

• Dyslexic students often omit **ed** endings even though they understand the grammatical concept of past-tense. That is why direct teaching of the sounds of ed is so useful.

Words for Reading and Dictation:

ed = /əd/ after t or d	ed = /d/	ed = /t/
twisted	smelled	jumped
planted	smiled	fished
rented	saved	skipped
mended	moved	asked
	handled	

More Advanced:

waited	rowed	slipped	scrapped
coasted	smelled	stepped	looked
shouted	seemed	snowed	turned

---

y

y₁
my /ī/
y₂
handy /ē/
y₃
gym /i/

y₁   y₂   y₃

Rule:
y = /ī/₁ /ē/₂ /i/₃   • Teach: M__y__ hand__y__ g__y__m.

Reading and Dictation:

cry	baby	gym	why	dirty	plywood
dry	funny	gypsum	try	bunny	Plymouth

Sentences for Dictation:

Pam can fly in the sky.   The gypsy is in the gym.
What a funny bunny!   The happy puppy jumps and barks.
My candy is in the gym.

• For advanced practice of **y** use word wheel. Refer to page 57.

Rule:

Divide a word between 2 consonants - **c/c**. The vowels will be short. Any syllable with this cvc pattern is called a closed syllable.

1. c/c

napkin	tandem	tinsel	anvil	upset
expel	victim	tonsil	gasket	index
admit	possum	rabbit	candid	hectic
confess	until	linden	talcum	sunset
gambit	nutmeg	public	submit	kitten
cuspid	quintet	hamlet	velvet	witness
happen	hiccup	tennis	cactus	gossip
wombat	attack	magnet	tidbit	bonnet
picnic	bandit	album	public	basket
humbug	goblin	compel	musket	

Accent:

This is a good place to begin work with accent. We need to teach accent directly. Have the student say the accent on each syllable in succession, and decide which way makes sense.

nap´kin

or

nap kin´

mag´net

or

mag net´

The student can learn to put the accent mark on the stressed syllable. See page 98 for additional teaching strategies.

Drill:

1. Tutor writes out a list of six or eight words in large print.
2. Present to student and have him/her draw a line between two consonants (nap/kin).
3. Student reads word aloud by syllables.
4. Tutor says, "Say it fast." Student says it fast, pulling the separate syllables into a word.

Phrases for Dictation:

velvet wombat	velvet basket	picnic tidbit
tin gasket	possum and kitten	
public witness	sunset and sunrise	

Sentences for Dictation:

The bandit had a musket.
The witness saw a rabbit.
The goblin had a hiccup.

Nonsense Sentences

Advanced:

Here are some nonsense sentences.

- Convat bram letfom.
- Bib sculp quimsat.
- Bogdat jums nivsig.
- Hanzad clob rasnult.
- Mun dit dulb vidlem.
- Rogdit bulfon fantrib.
- Proptem gop lospin rapsin.
- Frepmeg dultis septug claxtan.
- Crosmut vant colvent septude.
- Vagpot tomden ron gansad.

2. Consonant Blends

Words that contain consonant blends for syllable division practice.

expect	disturb	frantic	abrupt	fragment
publish	solvent	himself	encamp	triplets
plastic	engulf	children	trumpet	problem
connect	shipment	extend	plastic	tantrum
gumdrop	comment	object	traffic	
attach	advent	dentist		CONTINUED...

subject	insist	jonquil	problem	uplift
expand	suspend	disgust	dragnet	inflict
insect	pretzel	invent	expect	impact
contest	obstruct	contact	Tempest	channel
contract	consult	splendid	dentist	insult

2. Soft c and g

cancel	accept	forceps	stingy	cymbal	city
pungent	pencil	fancy	census	rancid	citrus

Drill:

Dictate a word by its syllables. The student repeats the word identifying the number of syllables. The student then writes the word saying the sounds as the sounds are written. Next, have the student read the word he or she has written, initially by its syllables then again quickly as a whole word. At the end of the exercise, after the words have been forgotten, have the student read the entire list.

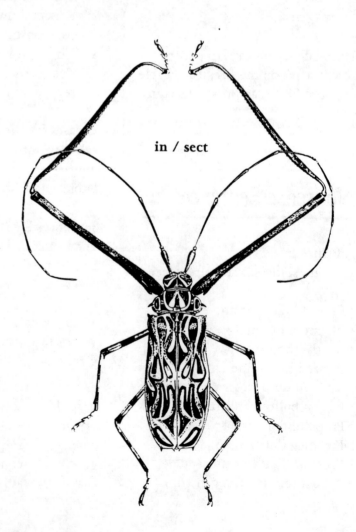

in / sect

"Don't ever, ever, ever worry about students being bored, as long as they'll do what you ask."
D.B.W.

a	a_1 apple /a.../ a_2 **apron** /$\bar{a}$/

e	e_1 Ed /e.../ e_2 **even** /$\bar{e}$/

i	i_1 it /i.../ i_2 **iron** /$\bar{i}$/

o	o_1 ox /o.../ o_2 **open** /$\bar{o}$/

u	u_1 up /u.../ u_2 **music** /yü/ u_3 **ruby** /$\overline{oo}$/

a_2 baby apron	e_2 recent even	i_2 silent iron
o_2 moment open	u_2 music unicorn	u_3 ruby

Rule:
- Long vowels commonly occur in open syllables.
- **Open syllables** are syllables that end with a vowel. The vowel is long.
- A long vowel says its name or a long vowel says the name of the letter. Note that long **u** always has two sounds /yü/ and /$\overline{oo}$/. The long vowel sounds of **y** are /$\bar{i}$/ and /$\bar{e}$/.

Open Syllables for Dictation and Reading:

si	va	e	cy	mo	ze	wa	so	re	pro
smu	de	mi	lo	de	dra	su	whi	cru	gly	vi
stri	gru	gy	yo	xy	ne	sha	cho	fa	hu	sy
di

"As soon as the students see how the foundation work carries over into everyday life, motivation will not be a problem."
D.B.W

Words that come in groups (common but irregular).

Rule:
Teach the student that words ending in **ld**, **st**, **nd**, and **lt** commonly have a single vowel with a long vowel sound.

comb	roll	mold	old
	troll	told	bold
	stroll	sold	cold
		scold	fold
			gold

bolt	bind	both	pint
colt	find	don't	mild
dolt	mind	won't	wild
jolt	wind	host	child
Holt	blind	most	blinds
molt	grind	post	minded
volt	hind	ghost	kindly
			kindness
			unkind
			behind
			blindfold
			remind

Sentences for Dictation and Reading:

This wild child is a troll.
Jane roped the colt to a brass post.
It is cold in winter.
Was it cold in summer also?
I combed the old, kind dog with a small comb.
I wish I had a pint of gold.
Hold the wild colt.

Hold the wild colt.

Rule:

If Rule # 1 doesn't work and there aren't two consonants in the middle of the word, then divide after the first vowel and make that vowel long (v̄/c). Any syllable ending in a long vowel is called an open syllable.

apron	iris	pony	chosen	tripod
baby	tulip	climax	lady	crisis
rival	tepee	rodent	music	bonus
raven	Friday	label	vocal	

Drill:

Write words in large print on a piece of paper. Have the student divide each word after the first vowel which is long and says its name. Next, have the student sound out the word by syllables. Finally, have the student say the whole word quickly.

Words to Divide and Read:

v̄/c - These words all follow syllable division rule #2. The first syllable is an open syllable with a long vowel /v̄/. The words are categorized according to sound and syllable concepts in the <u>final</u> syllables.

tripod	music	raven	biped	duplex
focus	pagan	Kodak	chosen	spoken
siphon	Jason	omit	Nobel	totem
rodent	open	silent	sinus	Salem
topaz	minus	apex	moment	evil
lotus	virus	Polish	student	motel
Poland	cement	cupid	elect	bonus
bacon	sedan	unit	relent	defend
propel	item	secret	humus	haven

y and silent e

canine	profile	require	polite
repose	provide	unite	refine
navy	reside	humane	feline
decide	tyrant	brocade	elate
baby	locate	behave	promote
secure	ozone	tirade	

Open syllables

hero	zero	negro	polo	solo

Soft c and g

silence	cyclone	recite	recycle	recent
recede	decent	gyroscope		

Accent:

Here is another good place to practice accent. Most but not all words that divide by Syllable Division Rule #2 have the accent on the first syllable as in:

ba´by
po´ny
vi̅´rus

Have the student say and divide the word and mark the accent.

Drill:

Have the student practice by dividing and reading aloud these words. The student should listen for long or short vowel sounds in the first syllables.

tulip	total	vocal	cotton	signal
digest	solo	student	happen	tunnel
pilot	rascal	ballot	omit	lesson
inhale	picnic	fifteen	basin	admit
publish	elect	bottom	local	oval
napkin	muffin	soda	public	velvet
locate	stampede	traffic	music	silent
polite	gossip	candy	invite	inside
unsafe	mistake	suppose	complete	dispose
basis	litmus	hotel	bobbin	sudden
consent	dentist	suspend	picnic	depend
sedan	disrupt	tempest	rabbit	hobnob
began	rattan	select	humbug	tandem
motel	tennis	pollen	victim	bonnet
bonus	cement	tablet	pulpit	fungus
minus	begin	escape		

rab / bit

Spelling Generalization

ck
duck /k/

> "Students need to compare and contrast in order to **hear** differences."
> D.B.W.

Note:
Before teaching this generalization be sure the student can hear the difference between short and long sounds of the vowels.

Rules:
ck: In spelling the final k, use ck at the end of one syllable words after a short vowel.
k: is used after a long vowel, one that says its own name.

Drill:
Dictate a word from each column. Have the student write words in correct columns. Be sure to make them **think** by varying the order of short and long vowels.

snack	snake	duck	Duke
back	bake	flack	flake
shack	shake	lick	like
pock	poke	lack	lake
Dick	dike	sack	sake
Spock	spoke	Mick	Mike
cock	Coke	lack	lake
black	Blake	tack	take
Mack	make	rack	rake
hack	hake	stack	stake
quack	quake	jock	joke
whack	wake	pick	pike
hick	hike	Jack	Jake

Note:
k: Is also used after a consonant. bank • milk • task • drink
c: Use c at the end of multisyllable words to spell /ik/. attic • cosmic • plastic • picnic

Words for practice:

neck	lock	metric	fleck	critic	optic
dusk	tannic	skeptic	tuck	trick	sulk
flank	track	sick	hectic	classic	rink
slink	aspic	check	frantic	deck	traffic
lank	hunk	stuck	mastic	mystic	speck

ang	sang
ing	sing
ong	song
ung	sung
ank	sank
ink	sink
onk	honk
unk	sunk

ang, ing, ong, ung, ank, ink, onk, unk
Use the ing, ang, card. The student may read from it.
e.g. ang-sang, ing-sing.

Words for Dictation:

ang	ing	ong	ung	ank	ink	onk	unk
gang	sing	bong	sung	tank	link	honk	lunk
hang	ming	gong	hung	sank	rink	bonk	hunk
rang	ring	long	dung	bank	sink	clonk	bunk
bang	ding	throng	lung	hank	wink		junk
sang	king	prong	rung	rank	mink		sunk
fang	ping	strong	tung	yank	kink		dunk
Tang	wing	song	slung	prank	fink		gunk
clang	sling	tong	stung	thank	slink		punk
swang	sting	Kong	strung	shank	drink		chunk
twang	swing		swung	shank	think		stunk
	thing		flung	crank	blink		spunk
	string			spank	clink		plunk
	bring			frank	plink		trunk
				stank	stink		shrunk
				drank	shrink		flunk
				clank	brink		slunk
				flank			
				blank			

"If a technique is good enough to use remedially, it is good enough to begin with."
Sylvia Richardson, M.D.
Past President, Orton Dyslexia Society

Sentences for Dictation:
The fish will shrink on the bank.
The shrimp will swim to the spring.
The strand in the string was strong.
The gong rang with a dong.
The throng drank from the spring.
Frank will think like a king.
Clang went the brass ring.
A string hung on the long trunk.
An ant stung the skunk.
Junk is in the dump.
The monk sang a long song.
Bang the gong so that it will clang.
Bring me a long strong string.
The mink went to the brink of the bank.
Swing on the plank of junk.
The man flung the dung.
The skunk stank.
A king had a Ding Dong and a Twinky.
King sat in the swing and swung.

ble, dle, fle... syllables

ble	table
dle	cradle
fle	rifle
gle	bugle
kle	sprinkle
tle	little
zle	puzzle
ple	apple

ble, dle, fle, gle, kle, tle, zle, ple

Drill:

This type of syllable always appears at the end of words. The vowel is silent and some dictionaries show the pronunciation: /b'l/, /d'l/, /f'l/ etc. The tutor may dictate from both lists for comparison.

Words for Dictation/Syllable Division Rule #1

cuddle	shingle	juggle	fumble	smuggle	trickle
paddle	crackle	stumble	turtle	fizzle	buckle
kettle	jingle	guzzle	gentle	baffle	freckle
dazzle	fickle	ripple	bottle	grapple	mingle
middle	tangle	circle	little	topple	wrinkle
riddle	ankle	icicle	rubble	settle	tickle
cattle	angle	pebble	sizzle	sniffle	pickle
waffle	bungle	giggle	drizzle	snuggle	cockle
saddle	chuckle	purple	battle	truffle	twinkle
tussle	freckle	bundle	bottle	hobble	spangle
wobble	single	throttle	little	fiddle	babble
apple	tumble	strangle	muffle	jungle	dribble
tangible	mangle	vegetable	eligible	scramble	brittle
hobble	ruffle	juggle	tackle	apple	straddle

Words for Dictation/Syllable Division Rule #2

ladle	table	Bible	cradle	bridle	title
noble	sable	gable	stable	maple	bugle
fable	trifle	rifle	stifle	idle	

Sentences for Dictation:

The table was stable.

The cattle were in the middle of the jungle.

The man with the freckles played the fiddle.

There is a single apple on the table.

The angle of the saddle made it wobble.

He ate a waffle with his pickle. Ugh!

She snuggled in the middle of the bed as she had a sniffle.

Her ankle hurt and she had to wobble on it.

He grappled with the puzzle as it baffled him.

Ladle the broth at the table.

The title of the book was the Bible.

The little table was unstable.

She had a bugle and a rifle.

Guzzle the bottle.

Stifle the giggle.

Handle the gentle cattle.

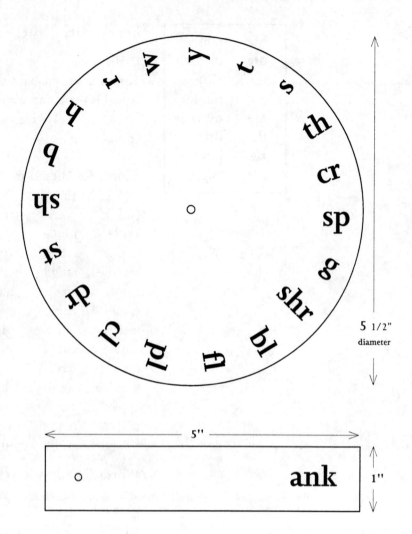

5 1/2"
diameter

←——— 5" ———→

ank   1"

■ The Round Word Wheel is an invaluable tool for intense practice in blending, decoding and syllable division.

Constructing the Round Word Wheel:

1. Cut out the pieces pictured above from poster board or simular heavy material. Cut out several pieces of each. You will find a template to follow in the appendix, page 121. You may tear out the template or you may choose to use a photocopy.

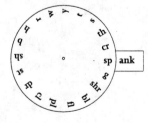

2. Attach the two pieces together with a brad so that the wheel turns freely.

3. Finally, with the wheel facing forward, ink in the letter patterns provided on the following page.

Round Word Wheel Letter Patterns

Use these round word wheel letter patterns or make up some of your own. Nonsense words are acceptable for decoding practice and are particularly useful for students who are "guessers".

Any word families may be used:
...ill, ...ack, ...ent, ...ick, ...ess, ...ell, ...ock, ...y, ...ore, ...ine, ...one, etc.

The following word patterns list word endings in **bold** letters at the top of columns. The columns list word beginnings which are written on the face of the Word Wheels.

ing	ang	ong	ung	ink	onk	unk	ank	y
sw	sw	cl	sl	l	h	ch	pr	b
st	d	g	str	p	l	st	th	bl
d	g	gl	br	r	p	sp	sh	br
l	h	l	s	dr	qu	h	cr	cl
m	r	m	m	th	r	j	sp	cr
t	b	pr	fl	bl	sh	l	fr	dr
y	sl	str	b	cl	shr	pl	pl	fl
r	s	thr	h	pl	thr	s	st	fr
s	r	b	d	st	b	tr	t	gl
k	f	pl	l	s	cl	b	s	gr
p	t	sp	r	w	dr	cl	b	pl
w	cl	fr	t	shr	ch	d	h	pr
sl	tw	s	sw	thr	d	shr	r	st
th	pl	t	st	b		fl	y	sl
str	str	k		cl		sl	dr	m
br				dr		g	cl	
				ch		p	fl	
				d			bl	

Round Word Wheel Letter Patterns (cont.)

Syllable Divison Rule #1

Word endings are in **bold** print.

ble		dle	fle	(g)le	(k)le	tle	zle	ple
crum	nim	trun	snif	gog	freck	net	puz	tem
drib	hob	fid	whif	jig	trick	tat	fiz	dim
grum	bob	pad	rif	gag	hack	rat	driz	ap
stum	bab	rid	raf	jug	fick	lit	noz	sam
thim	peb	han	muf	smug	cack	ket	daz	rip
trem	gob	mud	baf	stug	pick	bat		top
quib	am	spin	pif	squig	tack	shut		pim
rub	fum	cod	ruf	gig	crack	prat		sup
hum	rum	tod	shuf	gag	tick	whit		dap
gam	jum	can		hag	buck	bot		am
tum	wob	mid	**Rule #2**	wig	chuck	set		sim
ram	bub	pud	tri	sing	heck	cat		crip
dab		sad	sti	ting	knuck	scut		tip
		grid	ri	ming	brick	man		grap
		twid		bung	wrink			
Rule #2		strad		ang	tink			
sta	ca	fud		sang	crink			
fa	ta	bun		jang	rank			
bi	no	cud		mang				
sa	ru	**Rule #2**		spang				
ga	a	cra						
ma				**Rule #2**				
				bu				

Unphonetic Sight Words

Unphonetic sight words are words that cannot be "sounded out". These words must be memorized one at a time by all students for reading (spelling too if possible). It is helpful to place these words on flash cards. Be sure to review them as often as needed.

PREPRIMER	PRIMER	GRADE 1	GRADE 2	GRADE 3
a	are	again	been	carry
come	as	any	buy	does
one	do	could	does	done
said	four	give	don't	full
the	have	live	many	laugh
to	pretty	of	pull	only
two	there	once	their	small
where	they	put	very	
is	want	some	would	
	was	were	your	
	what	walk		
	who	know		

MISCELLANEOUS:

again	enough	heart	ocean	thorough
against	eye	height	often	though
also	February	honest	own	through
always	flood	hour	people	touch
among	floor	iron	pint	tough
answer	friend	island	prove	toward
beautiful	from	journey	pull	truth
blood	front	laugh	push	usual
build	goes	listen	rough	Wednesday
busy	gone	lose	says	whole
calf	gauge	love	sew	whom
clothes	guard	month	should	whose
cough	guess	money	son	wind
courage	guest	move	straight	wolf
debt	guide	muscle	sugar	won
door	guy	ninth	sure	worm
doubt	half	nothing	talk	

or /ōr/ for

"r-controlled" syllables are so called because the r following the vowel affects the sound of the vowel. Examples of "r controlled" syllables and pronunciations occurring in words appear on this and the following three pages.

Words for Dictation:

or	morn	torn	cornet	morning
for	cord	north	hornet	northern
nor	pork	short	order	morsel
sort	fork	forth	mortal	corridor
horn	lord	shorn	normal	border
form	worn	corner	horse	porch
cork	storm	ford	port	torch

Phrases for Dictation:

horn and torn
forlorn lord
pork chops
torn cord
sort of worn
short fork
a port in a storm

Sentences for Dictation:

Norman is my horse.
The porch faced north.
The horse was sort of worn.
The cork was short.
It was a normal morning.
There was a storm on the
    northern border.

ar /är/ car

Word for Dictation:

art	spar	barn	chart	scarf	garlic
arm	dart	lark	spark	march	tarnish
car	arch	dark	snarl	larch	artist
far	scar	mark	start	shark	discard
bar	darn	barb	harsh	starve	bombard
jar	card	yard	charm	large	harvest
tar	park	yarn	sharp	charge	party
mar	part	harm	stark	target	parch
cart	lard	farm	starch	armor	farmer

Sentences for Dictation:

Park the car at the arch.
A cart is in the yard.
Darn the sock with dark yarn.
Start the party in the park.
A large barn is on the farm.
Mark the chart with a star.
He has a scar on his arm.

Contrast:	
or	**ar**
for	far
corn	car
born	farm
fork	mar
sort	star

"r-controlled" vowels

er

her /ər/

er /ər/ her

Rule:
er, **ir**, and **ur** are all taught together as they can't be distinguished from one another auditorially. **er** is the most common spelling.

Words for Dictation:

her	perch	finger	silver
fern	under	tender	river
jerk	sister	permit	never
verb	winter	better	master
perk	number	whisper	November
herd	timber	whisker	monster
nerd	hunter	thunder	Robert
serf	enter	linger	Herbert
verse	hermit	singer	nerve
terse	summer	hammer	clerk
upper	bitter	dinner	

Phrases for Dictation:

summer or winter	tender finger
silver river	terse verse
number of whiskers	bitter winter
linger over dinner	

Sentences for Dictation:
The hunter went into the timber.
Her sister is on a perch under the fern.
The master is a hermit in the winter in December.

Contrast:

or	ar	er
cord	bar	her
lord	art	fern
cork	arm	verb
port	star	jerk
torn	arch	verse

Practice Phrase: Her bird is hurt.

ir /ər/ fir

Words for Dictation:

fir	birch	whirl	twirl	thirty	dirty
Sir	firm	third	swirl	smirk	confirm
girl	shirt	first	birth	whir	birthday
stir	chirp	dirt	thirst	bird	squirm

Phrases for Dictation:
first girl
dirty shirt
whirly bird
squirt for thirst
first and third birthdays
The bird will chirp in the fir.
She will twirl and whirl her skirt.
A squirrel is in a birch tree.
It was her third birthday.

Contrast:		
or	**ar**	**ir**
for	bar	fir
nor	Mark	girl
horn	lark	sir
lord	dark	bird
morn	bark	firm

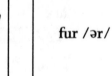

ur/ər/ fur

Words for Dictation:

cur	churn	hurry	surplus	slurp
fur	curse	furry	murder	blur
purr	burnt	curdle	burden	curb
curl	purse	purple	surprise	lurk
burn	nurse	turtle	turkey	blurt
turn	burst	hurdle	purpose	spur
hurt	burr	flurry	furnish	furnish
hurl	church	urchin	disturb	Saturn

Phrases for Dictation:
burn the logs
purple turtle
It was her first turn.
Sam jumped over the hurdle.
Murder the turkey.
Furnish the purpose.
Slurp the curdled buttermilk.
Do not disturb the church.
The urchin is in the surf.

Contrast:		
or	**ar**	**ur**
lord	yarn	cur
cord	Mark	fur
Ford	farm	turn
torn	part	hurt
port	lard	blur

Vowels with "r" can have irregular sounds. It is not necessary to teach these for memorization. The categories are given for awareness and explanation for the student and tutor. In an unaccented syllable, the vowel becomes a **schwa** /ə/ or /u/ sound.

or /ər/ schwa		ar /ār/	
doctor	author	arrow	carrot
visitor	sailor	barren	carry
mayor	error	parallel	marry
worm	world	charity	parrot
worry	work		

ar /ər/ schwa		ar /ōr/	
dollar	beggar	war	wart
lizard	coward	warn	warm
standard	custard	swarm	warden
collar	popular	award	reward

In these words **er** and **ir** all occur in accented syllables and have a more definite sound than schwa.

er /ār/		ir /ir/
errand	very	spirit
error	America	irrigate
peril	terrier	irregular
merry	inherit	irritate
merit	prosperity	mirror

ear /ər/ schwa		ear /ār/
early	pearl	wear
earn	Earl	bear
earnest	earth	tear
learn	search	pear
heard		swear

a

a₁
apple /a/

a₂
baby /ā/

a₃
wall /o/ /ä/

The walrus is on the water.

a₃ /o/ or /ä/ wall

Rule:
Use after **w** or before **l**.

Words for Dictation:

wall	wand	walk	wash	water	wander
wad	talk	want	watt	wasp	walrus
halt	swat	call	warm	chalk	swamp
salt	swab	malt	wallet	walnut	always

Review spelling rule ff, ll, ss, zz.

all	hall	call	tall	small
ball	fall	wall	mall	stall

Sentences for Dictation:
All the salt is in the dish.
We went for a walk and a talk.
Hit the ball on the wall.
Did Carl fall from the tall tree?
Jack lost his wallet on the walk.

Advanced:
ough /o/ /ä/ bought
augh /o/ /ä/ caught

Words for Dictation:

taught	sought
daughter	fought
naughty	brought
slaughter	thought

Sentences for Dictation:
He caught the ball.
She brought water.
She taught her naughty
daughter to be good.

Note:
Western speakers do not usually distinguish between the vowel sounds in **c**o**t** and **ca**ught. Therefore, in this manual the /o/ and /ä/ will be used for these and for a₃. Easterners definitely do distinguish between **o** and **au** and this could cause confusion.

tion

	tion station /shun/

tion /shun/ station

Words for Dictation:

ration	friction	nation	invitation	direction
lotion	faction	question	vacation	digestion
mention	fiction	quotation	solution	connection
potion	section	suction	objection	auction
motion	fraction	attention	correction	position
station	action	traction	foundation	aquisition

sion

	sion₁ mission /shun/

sion₁ /shun/ mission

Words for Dictation:

tension	compulsion	compression	suspension
extension	propulsion	submission	
expansion	confession	oppression	

sion

	sion₁ mission /shun/ sion₂ division/zhun/

sion₂ /zhun/ division

Words for Dictation:

television	decision	explosion	abrasion
occasion	seclusion	excursion	collision
intrusion	invasion	provision	exclusion
division	fusion	conclusion	aversion

Sentences for Dictation:

This is my favorite television station.
It always has action and motion.
I watch it on every occasion.
We need good traction.
Jan has good vision.
Her invitation was a good diversion.
My decision is to take a vacation.

Note: _____
tion and **sion** are word endings. When you hear a /shun/ and are in doubt as to whether to spell it tion or sion, use tion as it is more common.

Note: _____
ci and **ti** are sometimes pronounced /sh/ in final syllables. Examples...

ci
social	spacious
racial	musician
special	electrician
delicious	physician
precious	conscious
conscience	

ti
partial
patient
substantial
potential
ambitious

Rule part 1:   1-1-1-1
When the following conditions are met, double the final consonant in a word when adding an ending (suffix.) The base word must have one syllable, ending in one consonant after one short vowel and the suffix must begin with one vowel. If any of these conditions is **not** met, then don't double. Don't double with -ful, -ly, -ment, -ness. Doubling consonants keeps the vowel short.

Remember the 1-1-1-1 rule.
1- Does the base word have **one** syllable?
1- Does the base word end in **one** consonant...
1- after **one** short vowel?
1- Does the suffix begin with **one** vowel?
If these conditions are met, double the final consonant in the base word.

Examples:
ship + er = shipper
111 + 1 ..... all rules apply therefore the p is doubled.

ship + ment = shipment
111 + NO ...... consonant starting suffix.

needing + ing = needing
11 NO .... two vowels.

cold + er = colder
1 NO .... base word ends in two consonants.

The following **"code"** reminder may be written at the top of a practice page when drilling.

Does the base word have
    ...**1** syllable?
    ...**1** consonant at end?
    ...**1** short vowel?
Does the suffix begin with
    ...**1** vowel?

Drill: ───────────────────

hot + est = _hottest_		drop + ing, ed = _____
slop + y = _____		chop + ing, ed = _____
star + y = _____		skip + ed, ing = _____
swim + ing = _____		fat + est, er = _____
wit + ness = _____		fog + ed, y = _____
cold + er = _____		ship + ing, ed = _____
bad + ly = _____		big + er, ness = _____
hop+ ing = _____		cook + ing, ed = _____
blot + er = _____		bus + ing, ed = _____
weed + ing = _____		trim + ed, ing = _____
grit + y = _____		rain + ing, y = _____
jump + ing = _____		cool + ness, ing = _____
grin + ing = _____		sleep + er, ing = _____
rest + less = _____		pack + ed, ing = _____

Doubling Rule part 2

Doubling Rule part 2:   1-1-1
In words of more than one syllable, if the accent is on the final
syllable and that syllable ends in one consonant after one short
vowel, double the final consonant before a suffix beginning
with a vowel.

Remember the 1-1-1 rule.
If a base word has more than one syllable, first check that the
last syllable carries the accent, then apply the 1-1-1 rule.

Is the accent on the last syllable?
1- Does the last syllable end in **one** consonant...
1- after **one** short vowel?
1- Does the suffix begin with **one** vowel?
If these conditions are met, double the final consonant.

Examples:
admit´ + ance = admittance... accent is on the end syllable
pi´lot + ing = piloting... accent isn't on the end syllable

"Code" reminder Part 2

Does the last syllable have
        ...the accent?
        ...**1** consonant at end?
        ...**1** short vowel?
Does the suffix begin with
        ...**1** vowel?

Drill: ─────────────────────────────
Student says the base word and places the accent, then the
ending following the doubling line. A "code" reminder may
be written at the top of a practice page.

forgot´+ en = __forgotten__   begin + er = _____
    incur + ed = _____   + ing = _____
    limit + ed = _____   travel + er = _____
    disbar + ed = _____   + ing = _____
    profit + able = _____   open + ed = _____
blunder + ing = _____   + ing = _____
market + able = _____   transmit + er = _____
    shovel + ing = _____   + ing = _____
    patrol + ed = _____   + ed = _____
    litter + ing = _____   submit + ing = _____
                                                + ed = _____
                                            recur + ing = _____
                                                + ence = _____

*"Teach by questioning. Keep the tutor talk to a
minimum. The student should have a maxi-
mum of response,"*
D.B.W.

Rule:
The purpose of the **e** in silent e words is to make the vowel long. When adding a suffix that begins with a vowel, the silent e is dropped and the vowel remains long.

Examples:
blame + ing = blaming
blame + less = blameless

Drill: _____

drop + ed = _____	skip + ed = _____
mend + ed = _____	step + ed = _____
hope + ing = _____	hide + ing = _____
hope + ful = _____	hope + ed = _____
dine + ing = _____	lone + ly = _____
write + ing = _____	use + ful = _____
tune + ful = _____	sure + ly = _____
shine + y = _____	cure + ed = _____
time + er = _____	close + ed = _____
sore + ness = _____	ride + ing = _____
flame + ing = _____	hide + ing = _____
care + ing = _____	make + ing = _____
dive + ing = _____	slope + ing = _____
shade + y = _____	slime + y = _____
noise + less = _____	life + less = _____
tire + some = _____	like + ness = _____
safe + er = _____	educate + ing = _____
safe + ty = _____	inhale + ed = _____
cute + est = _____	twinkle + ing = _____
provide + ing = _____	manage + ing = _____
complete + ed = _____	sincere + ly = _____
trim + ed = _____	settle + ment = _____
grab + ed = _____	smell + ed = _____
unite + ed = _____	grant + ed = _____

"Treat people as if they were what they ought to be, and you help them become what they are capable of being."
Goethe

Note:
Teach two words for the doubling or silent e rule i.e. hop and hope. Say, "Is it a word like hop? If so, then double. Is it a word like hope? Then don't double."

Comparing Doubling Rule and Silent e Rule

For Reading:
If you <u>see</u> two consonants together, use a short vowel sound. If you <u>see</u> a single consonant, use a one vowel sound.

For Spelling:
If you <u>hear</u> a short vowel, double the consonant. If you <u>hear</u> a long vowel, write one consonant.

Put the following words on a tachistoscope for reading practice. See the following page for instructions to make a tachistoscope. Dictate them for spelling. If a student has difficulty, review the syllable division rules #1 and #2.

capped	filling	matter
caper	filed	matting
capping	filing	mated
sitting	filled	biting
sitter	skidding	bitter
sited	bidding	biter
slipper	bidder	scared
slipping	hiding	scarred
sloping	hidden	scaring
sloppy	taping	scarring
sloped	tapping	ripping
slopping	taped	riper
sliding	tapped	ripped
skating	tapper	riding
moping	mating	ridding
mopping	matter	ridden
mopped	cutter	rider
slimming	cuter	shipping
slimy	cutting	shaping
slimmer	hopped	shaper
shining	hoped	coping
shinning	hopping	copper
shinned	hoping	
shiny	hopper	

Drill:
Join these words and suffixes.

ripe + er
ripe + ness
rip + ing
rip + ed
slop + ing
slope + ing
slope + ed
slop + y
shop + ing
shop + ed
scrub + ing
dive + ing
milk + ed
pop + ing
mad + ness
haze + y
hop + ing
hop + ed
hope + ing
hid + en

Drill:
Compare the following: read, and write from dictation.

hoping _____ hopping
filed _____ filled
sloping _____ sloppy
sliding _____ slipped
moping _____ mopping
ripped _____ ripen
hiding _____ hidden
mating _____ matting
biting _____ bitter
riding _____ ridding
taped _____ tapped

ch

ch₁
chin /ch/
ch₂
Christmas /k/

ch₂ /k/ Christmas

Words for Dictation:

school	echo	stomach	Christ
ache	technical	chorus	bronchitis
choir	chrome	chrysalis	chronicle
character	chronological		

"Our goal is mastery of print. When students don't have to be told the words, it gives them a sense of power."
D.B.W.

Chameleons go to school.

Schwa:
In an unaccented syllable, the vowel sound is often swallowed and becomes an /u/ as in up. This is called a schwa /ə/.

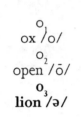

a₁	apple /a/
a₂	baby /ā/
a₃	all /ȯ//ä/
a₄	banana /ə/

a₄ /ə/ banana

Vowel in unaccented syllable: ba na´na

along	ago	awake	bridal	alike
awake	amuse	local	normal	floral
mortal	canal	cadet	caress	China

o₁	ox /o/
o₂	open /ō/
o₃	lion /ə/

o₃ /ə/ lion

love	glove	ton	money	other

Vowel in unaccented syllable:

beckon	bottom	cannon	carbon	Boston	kingdom

i /ə/   Less common, therefore do not put it on the i card.

muffin	victim	denim	cabin	pencil	bobbin
pupil	robin	stupid			

e /ə/   Less common, therefore do not put it on the e card.

kitten	bitten	stiffen	sudden	towel	kennel
camel	burden	pocket	velvet	vessel	trumpet

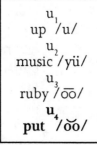

u₁	up /u/
u₂	music /yü/
u₃	ruby /o͞o/
u₄	put /o͝o/

u₄ /o͝o/ put

bushes	pull	push	bush
bushel	pully	full	bull

Sentences for Dictation:
The pussy cat sits on a cushion.
Jan has a cupful of pudding.
The bullet is in the gun.
Push that bushel aside.

Rule:
If rule #2 doesn't work, make the vowel short and move the dividing line after the consonant. (**vc/**)

Drill:
Have the pupil use the syllable division rules in order, first Rule #1, then if there are no consonants together, try Rule #2. If the word doesn't make sense, then try Rule #3. Most words will divide up by these three rules.

cam/el	satin	robin	sever	seven	cabin	visit
sev/en	banish	lemon	model	atom	colic	profit
ref/uge	denim	habit	medal	solid	pedal	static
valid	closet	level	gamin	gavel	polish	potash
gravel	spinet	talent	relic	tribune	relish	havoc
tonic	refuge	comic	granule	comet	planet	tepid
bodice	talon	frolic	timid	second	punish	venom
mimic	panel	famish	modest	salad	rapid	

- Use laminated list cards or copy words onto a list.
- These words can be used for more practice in placing accent. Words divided according to rule #3 have the accent on the first syllable.
- Remember that in **unaccented syllables**, the vowel often makes a schwa /ə/ or /u/ sound.

Syllable Division Rule #1, #2, & #3

Syllable Division Rules:
The purpose of the syllable division rules is to improve reading decoding and spelling. We want students to be able to take words apart and change the vowel sounds.
Heaven forbid that a student would go through life thinking Rule #1, Rule #2 and Rule #3.

Use the three rules of syllable division. **c/c   v̄/c   vc/**

gob/lin	pendulum	spider	advantage
de/cide	molasses	iris	over
spat/ter	feverish	cabin	visit
level	important	cucumber	murmur
locate	inspector	fantastic	lemon
infect	nutmeg	represent	absent
spoken	punish	regulate	compete
silent	crisis	ignorant	octopus
truly	pepper	buffalo	elastic
fever	focus	digest	horizon
fortune	scalpel	pilot	mercury
omit	illegal	student	occupant
ornate	lady	muffin	unbroken
mistake	trumpet	umpire	remit

Advanced:
- Divide the following words by syllable division rules, 1, 2, and 3.
- Remember that in unaccented syllables the vowel often makes a schwa sound /ə/ even though it occurs in an open syllable and by the rule would be a long vowel. e.g. dynamo dy'nə mo'.
- Place the accent on the stressed syllable. This helps pronunciation.
- For spelling: Do not use the schwa sound. Emphasize the short or long sound of the vowel in pronunciation so the student can spell the word correctly.

rich/ness	election	entrust	compromise	dethrone
con/dense	inhuman	reprint	statement	painful
enrichment	disgraceful	enslavement	unmindful	retirement
entanglement	uneventful	favorable	servant	different
inhabitant	continent	preferable	unmanageable	contestant
removable	unpardonable	informant	unobservant	respective
electrical	political	dismissal	progressive	restorative
accumulate	history	advantage	surrender	impolite
porcupine	corporal	tomato	professor	accustom
torpedo	comprehend	admittance	ambulance	bulletin
independent	circulate	incubator	elastic	indignant
lumbago	pendulum	tornado	gymnastics	carpenter
mercury	important	buffalo	passenger	acrobat
gorilla	harmonize	volcano	potato	romantic
gyroscope	dynamite	diplomat	calculate	democracy
hibernate	dictator	horizon	innocent	yesterday
sarcastic	emergency	argument	abdomen	commando
establish	occupy	domestic	occupant	represent
kindergarten	tobacco	percolate	equator	tuberculosis
suffocate	alcohol	chimpanzee	consonant	victory
tonsillitis	balcony	republic	spectator	dynamo
turpentine	cucumber	hypnotism	mandolin	entertain
committee	factory	revolver	supervise	octopus
advertise	molasses	misfortune	importune	interfere
undermine	interpose	confiscate	vanquish	infantile
infant	telegraph	consequence	evacuate	confuse
atmosphere	alphabet	intended	educate	seclude
invasion	devote	compress	extension	pretend
grapple	cradle	purple	scramble	vehicle
mandolin	interlude	electric	tremble	episode
hippodrome	introduce	solitude	fabricate	evaluate
museum	granulate	investigate	reproduce	manicure
platinum	regulation	reproduction	dictate	dictation
hospital	explanation	admire	admiration	promote
promotion	pervade	triumphant	sarcastic	ventilate
everglade	minimum	recognize	regulate	operate

tch

tch
catch /ch/

"The learning curve doesn't just go up, it plateaus.
Learning sometimes needs to "simmer".
D.B.W.

tch /ch/ catch

Rules:

ch Use **ch** at the beginning of a word and at the end of a word after a consonant, as in **ch**in and lun**ch**.

tch Use **tch** after a short vowel as in ma**tch**.
Exceptions: rich, which, such, much, sandwich.

Words for Practice:

chop	porch	ditch	scratch	Scotch	bench
hatch	French	batch	thatch	lunch	pinch
stretch	hitch	church	blotch	latch	chill
sketch	witch	branch	fetch	patch	church
Dutch	clutch	retch	starch	chest	pitch
lurch	thatch	hutch	stitch	splotch	

Sentences for Dictation:
Pitch the tent.
He spilled his lunch.
Starch the french dress.
Patch the ditch by the church.
Will you pitch if I catch?
Fetch the batch of French gems.

Compare and Contrast	
ch	**tch**
chill	batch
chop	crutch
pinch	ditch
branch	retch
lunch	hatch
chunk	scotch

Watch the chick hatch.

dge /j/ **fudge**

dge

dge
fudge /j/

Rules:

dge Use after a short vowel when you hear a /**j**/ sound at the end of the word.

ge Use after a consonant or after a long vowel.

Words for Practice:

badge	lodge	sludge	sledge	fudge	bridge
judge	hedge	edge	dodge	ridge	budge
dredge	smudge	ledge	wedge	grudge	trudge

age	huge	strange	change	cage	page
hinge	rage	sage	stage	gage	wage
loge	barge	large	urge	gorge	plunge
serge	forge	range	verge	ledger	stranger

Phrases and Sentences for Dictation:

hodge-podge

strange bridge

a large lodge

huge ridge

edge of the stage

Change the cage.

Trudge on the stage.

The judge has a huge badge.

Plunge in the hedge.

*"School **is** reading. Therefore, any child who fails in reading is bound to be upset."*
D.B.W.

Compare and Contrast	
dge	**ge**
badge	page
edge	rage
lodge	loge
fudge	forge
ledge	huge
Madge	wage

oa
boat /ō/

Vowel Team Syllables:
Words and syllables containing vowel combinations are called vowel team syllables or words.

oa /ō/ boat

Drill:
For spelling emphasize: **oa** in the middle of a word.

Words for Dictation:

boat	throat	Joan	oak	boast	coat
croak	loan	soak	roast	goat	roach
goal	cloak	coast	moat	coach	coal
groan	loaf	float	groan	goal	toad
goal	road	moan	oath	soap	coax

Phrases for Dictation:

poach an egg	Loaf on the coast.
hop toad	Toast the loaf.
an oak boat	Soak in the foam.
moan and groan	Float the boat in the moat.
Coast on the road.	Load the float, Joan.

The coach has a croak in his throat.

oe
toe /ō/

oe /ō/ toe

Drill:
For spelling emphasize: **oe** usually at the end of words.

Words for Dictation:

toe   woe   roe   Joe   hoe   foe   doe   Moe

Phrases for Dictation:

big toe	Moe hurt his toe.
fish roe	Joe has a foe.
Woe is me.	Tiptoe with a hoe.

ee
feet /ē/

ee /ē/ feet

ee usually occurs in the middle of words.

Words for Dictation:

eel	feed	jeep	fleet	screech
fee	reef	tree	street	street
bee	deep	teem	steep	green
wee	heel	flee	steel	queer
feel	peek	three	sweep	screem
seed	beet	bleed	teeth	weekend
feet	meet	greed	sleep	sixteen
week	keep	beech	creep	fifteen
peel	beef	greet	cheek	indeed

Phrases and Sentences for Dictation:

green tree	Feed the tree.
steel wheel	Three sheep had wee feet.
steep street	Peek and see the screen.
fleet street	Peel the beet.
heels on the feet	I need to keep the jeep
beef and beets	Greet the fleet with a speech.
Sweep the street.	The beech tree is green.
Greet the Queen.	Creep up the street.

"Any child can be taught to read commensurate with his ability to think."
Margaret Rawson
Past Editor
Orton Society Bulletin

The three sheep had wee feet.

ai

ai
sail /ā/

Feed the grain to the quail.

ai /ā/ sail

Words for Dictation:

fail	strain	stair	chain	gain	airmail
ail	main	rail	brain	stain	airport
mail	aid	tail	trait	grain	airship
sail	laid	wail	waist	plain	airsick
aim	maid	quail	faith	stair	hairpin
hail	raid	snail	waif	pain	haircut
bait	air	trail	lair	main	quaint
wait	fair	frail	rain	Spain	braid
pail	hair	flair	vain	train	mailbox
train	chair	drain	plain	paint	mailman

Sentences for Dictation:
Wail on the trail for the quail.
Have faith in the mailman.
Chain the sail to the main mast.
Paint the chair and the stairs.
The sprain was a pain.
The rain fell on the quaint train.
Feed the grain to the quail.
The rain in Spain fell on the plain.

ay

ay
ay /ā/

ay /ā/ say

Rule:
For spelling, teach "when you **hear** an /ā/ at the end of a word spell it **ay**; when you hear an /ā/ in the middle of the word spell it **ai**."

Words for Dictation:

bay	May	pay	slay	pray	delay
day	gay	way	dray	clay	repay
may	hay	jay	gray	play	getaway
nay	lay	sway	tray	stray	railway
Fay	say	stay	fray	away	haystack

Phrases for Dictation:

railway train	Ray lay in the hay stack.
spray the tray	Pay the way for May and Fay.
May ran away.	It's a gray day.

oi
boil /oi/

oi /oi/ oil

Words for Dictation:

boil	soil	coin	voice	rejoice
coil	toil	hoist	loin	embroil
roil	moist	noise	toilet	loiter
point	joist	noisy	moisture	oilcloth
foist	avoid	groin	ointment	embroider
choice	void	joint	goiter	exploit
poise	oil	broil	devoid	turmoil
foil	spoil	poison	poinsettia	thyroid

Phrases for Dictation:
Hoist up the sail.
Put oil in the joint.
Boil the egg in oil.
Poison will spoil the soil.
A hip is a joint at the top of the leg.
A car needs gas and oil.
Noise annoys me.
Broil with soy while moist.
I enjoy the voyage.
Do not spoil his joy with toil.

oy
boy /oi/

oy /oi/ boy

Rule:
For spelling teach "when you **hear** an /oi/ at the end of a word spell it **oy**, when you hear an /oi/ in the middle of the word spell it **oi**."

Words for Dictation:

boy	Troy	royal	boycott	deploy
Roy	soy	oyster	destroy	viceroy
toy	ploy	annoy	cowboy	soybean
coy	cloy	enjoy	loyal	voyage
joy	alloy	employ	royalty	flamboyant

Phrases for Dictation:

Roy had a toy train.	Enjoy the royalty.
Troy is a joy.	Don't be coy.

OO

oo₁
food /o͞o/

Practice Phrase: Food is good.

oo₁ /o͞o/ food

Words for Dictation:

too	cool	loose	spoon	croon	gloom
coo	loot	hoot	gloom	moose	brood
zoo	tooth	noose	troop	soon	stooge
roof	boot	spook	loop	shoot	groove
food	loose	school	broom	whoop	shampoo
room	droop	spool	groom	droop	Kalamazoo

Sentences for Dictation:

Tom has a loose tooth.
The cook will stir with a cool spoon
The noose for the moose was loose.
The crook stole the loot.
The three stooges went to the zoo.
A spook shook in the moon light.
Jim will brood in the gloomy wood.
The school has a loose roof.
Soon the room will be cool.

OO

oo₁
food /o͞o/
oo₂
good /o͝o/

The goose is good.

oo₂ /o͝o/ good

Words for Dictation:

poor	look	book	cook	hook	shook
foot	good	took	hood	stood	brook
wool	wood	soot	rook	crook	good-bye

Phrases for Dictation:

Mom is a good cook.
Tom has a wool sock on his foot.
Jim shook the poor cook.
He stood on one foot by the brook.
He had a good book to look at.
He has soot on his hood.
Bob has a fish on the hook.

OW ow₁ plow /ou/

Practice Phrase: Plow the snow.

ow₁ /ou/ plow

Words for Dictation:

sow	vow	shower	flower	prow
cow	now	chowder	allow	drowsy
owl	brow	down	bowel	prowl
how	brown	howl	chow	towel
bow	scow	scowl	fowl	rowdy
frown	crown	clown	however	pow-wow
vowel	plow	crowd	trowel	endowment
power	powder	gown	jowl	dowel

Sentences for Dictation:

How the owl howls.
He ate the clam chowder.
Plow the flower garden.
How now brown cow?
The clown had a brown brow.

Milk the brown cow.
We will go downtown.
Let's not frown and scowl.
The power of the shower
 helps the flowers.

OW ow₁ plow /ou/ ow₂ snow /ō/

ow₂ /ō/ snow

Words for Dictation:

throw	bow	row	blow	flown	thrown
flow	low	slowly	flow	grown	bowl
crow	slow	mow	grown	below	snowball
glow	rowboat	sow	own	shown	grown
snow	tow	growth	owner	owe	rainbow

Sentences for Dictation:

The snow blows.
The ball was thrown slowly.
Tow the boat by the bow.
The owner throws the snowball.
Make the fire glow by blowing on it.
Show me how the cow has grown.
He owns the bowl.
Sow the row with seeds.
The rooster crowed in the glow of day.

ie

ie₁
piece /ē/

Practice Phrase: piece of pie

ie₁ /ē/ piece

Words for Dictation:

field	belief	reprieve	siege	fierce	thief
piece	believe	grief	priest	pierce	retrieve
chief	grieve	niece	tier	shriek	
brief	relieve	shield	pier	achieve.	

Sentences for Dictation:
You have a piece of the field.
A shriek will achieve a shock.
The priest believes in God.
Grieve to relieve your sadness.
Grief has a brief reprieve.
Retrieve the shield.
I believe in the chief.

ie

ie₁
piece /ē/
ie₂
pie /ī/

ie₂ / ī/ pie

Words for Dictation:

die	pie	tie	lie	fie	vie
belie	underlie				

Sentences for Dictation:
I could die for some pie.
He wore a red tie.
The log lies in the fire.

ou

ou₁	out /ou/

Practice Phrase: out of soup

ou₁ / ou/ out

Words for Dictation:

out	ouch	tout	scowl	flour	thousand
foul	loud	about	mouth	scout	founder
rout	tout	south	couch	snout	pouch
crouch	ounce	pounce	grout	sour	flounder
stout	trout	sprout	slouch	bounce	thou
grouch	count	fount	pound	house	noun
mount	mound	proud	cloud	grouse	snout
shroud	ground	found	hound	pout	sound
round	wound	gout	spout	vouch	abound

Sentences for Dictation:
Get a pound of ground round.
He found the wet ground on the mound.
The stout hound was a scout.
Put the couch in the house.
Shout when you pound.
Do not slouch on the couch.
Ouch! My mouth hurts and makes me a grouch.
The trout wound himself around the line.
The proud scout was in the round house.
The waves pounded on the sand with a loud sound.

ou

ou₁	out /ou/
ou₂	soup /o͞o/

ou₂ /o͞o/ soup

Words for Dictation:

soup	wound	youth	soupy	group

Sentences for Dictation:
Don't let the hot soup wound you!
The youth joined the group.

au

au
August
/o/ /ä/

au /o/ /ä/ August

Rule:
For spelling, **au** is never at the end of a word.

Words for Dictation:

August	auto	fault	because	vault	jaunt
haul	Paul	vault	laundry	saunter	haunt
aunt	cause	pause	jaunty	sausage	sauce
audit	jaunt	faucet	gaudy	saucer	launch
laud	taut	daunt			

Sentences for Dictation:
Paul will do his laundry in August.
The saucer was under the Aunt's faucet.
I am not daunted by the sauce for the sausage.
My auto will not have a fault that makes it pause.
The audit showed the cause was fraud.
Saul has gaudy laundry.

aw

aw
saw /o/ /ä/

aw /o/ /ä/ saw

Words for Dictation:

raw	hawk	dawn	claw	yawn
straw	saw	awe	thaw	lawyer
squaw	awful	jaw	awl	law
scrawl	slaw	draw	drawn	paw

Sentences for Dictation:
I saw his awful claw in the dawn.
Our lawyer scrawls.
I'm in awe of the straw hawk.
The jaw of the squaw was drawn in a yawn.
The dog's paw was raw after the thaw.
Do you like cole slaw?

ea

ea₁
eat /ē/

Practice Phrase: Eat bread and steak.

ea₁ /ē/ eat

Words for Dictation:

ear	feast	weak	teach	bean	reap
tea	wheat	leaf	squeak	reach	cheap
seat	dream	east	meat	least	seat
year	yeast	bead	leak	peach	mean
each	stream	leap	read	feast	sneak
rear	beach	clear	peak	streak	beast
dear	sea	clean	heal	steam	lean
team	real	speak	heap	treat	real
peak	tear	reach	meal	fear	

Phrases and Sentences for Dictation:

weak tea	We eat meat for a treat at a meal.
cheap beach	Teach me how to eat a peach.
clean beast	Dream each year for a peak team.
real meat	The cheap dress has a weak seam.
peaches and cream	Sneak up the beach to the stream.

ea₂ /e/ bread

ea

ea₁
eat /ē/

ea₂
bread /e/

Words for Dictation:

dead	weather	healthy	spread	instead
lead	death	weather	breath	jealous
deaf	weapon	heavy	leather	wealthy
dread	threaten	read	heaven	breakfast
sweat	ready	bread	pleasant	ahead
thread	steady	thread	dreadful	sweater
feather	meadow	threat	already	

Phrases and Sentences for Dictation:

pleasant breakfast	Get ready for the cold weather.
feather bed	Eat a healthy breakfast.
dreadful sweater	Wear a heavy leather jacket.
bread spread	It is dreadful to be jealous.

ea₃ /ā/ steak

ea

ea₁
eat /ē/

ea₂
bread /e/

ea₃
steak /ā/

Words for Dictation:

break	breaks	great	steak	greatest	daybreak

Phrases and Sentences for Dictation:

great steak	The sun comes out at daybreak.
greatest break	Break out that great beef steak.

ey

ey
valley /ē/

ey /ē/ valley

Rule:

ey is at the end of words, but it is not common.
Exceptions to ey /ā/ obey, grey, prey, they, and hey.

Words for Dictation:

alley   valley   honey   money   jockey   key
monkey   turkey   journey   chimney

Sentences for Dictation:

The gate leads to the alley.   The turkey stood on the donkey.
Do you have any money?   The monkey was in the alley.
I like honey on my bread.   The donkey went on a journey.

The monkey likes honey.

igh

**igh
high /ī/**

igh /ī/ high

Words for Dictation:

high	higher	thigh	lightning	night	sunlight
light	highway	might	moonlight	tight	overnight
flight	flashlight	sight	tonight	fright	frighten
right	delights	frighten	midnight	tighten	lighten
slight	mighty	bright	brightness	highest	brighten
sigh	highness	highly	lighthouse	insight	limelight

Phrases for Dictation:

bright moonlight	right highway
high delight	lighten the load
midnight moonlight	frighten the dog
bright sunlight	slightly higher
mighty tight	delight her highness
lightning at midnight	good insight

Sentences for Dictation:
The moonlight is bright tonight.
Turn on the light at night.
The sunlight is mighty bright.
I don't need a flashlight.
Fix the rope tightly on the highest tree.

eigh

**eigh
eight /ā/**

eigh /ā/ eight

Words for Dictation:

weight	neigh	weigh	neighborhood
sleigh	eight	freight	eighty-eight
neighbor	eighty	eighteen	

Sentences for Dictation:
She is eighty-eight years old.
The sleigh was pulled by eight horses.
My neighbor hauls freight.
What is your weight?
I weigh too much!
Her house is the eighth in the neighborhood.

ue₁ /o͞o/ true

Words for Dictation:

due rue subdue pursue avenue glue
blue flue true construe misconstrue.

ue₂ /yü/ rescue

Words for Dictation:

hue cue virtue issue rescue continue
statue argue tissue

Phrases and Sentences for Dictation:

rue the day	The glue is due.
blue hue	The flue is open.
argue and sue	The avenue continues.
Rescue the statue.	Her virture is true.
Pursue the cue.	Don't miscontrue my meaning.
Issue the tissue.	She used a blue tissue.

ue₁ true /o͞o/

ue₁ true /o͞o/
ue₂ rescue /yü/

Practice Phrase: true rescue

ew₁ /yü/ few

Words for Dictation:

ewe mew hew curfew nephew pewter

ew₂ /o͞o/ grew

Words for Dictation:

blew chew crew drew grew threw
pew news dew mildew new renew
stew newspaper

Phrases and Sentences for Dictation:

few grew	He threw away the pewter plate.
new stew	There was mildew on the pew.
Renew the newspaper.	Her nephew chewed gum.
He blew on the stew.	The new crew worked hard.
Dew is on the new grass.	Chew your food well.

ew₁ few /yü/

ew₁ few /yü/
ew₂ grew /o͞o/

Practice Phrase: few plants grew

ei

ei₁ veils /ā/

ei₁ /ā/ veils

Words for Dictation:
vein   rein   veil   heir   skein   their
reindeer   surveillance

Sentences for Dictation:
Santa came with his sleigh.
Joan weighs a lot at eighteen years of age.
Hold the reins for the eighth time.
The skein of yarn is red.
The Muslim woman wore a veil.

ei

ei₁ veils /ā/
ei₂ deceive /ē/

ei₂ /ē/ deceive

Words for Dictation:
ceiling   conceit   seize   receive   seizure   deceit
receipt   neither   perceive   conceive   either   deceive
weird   leisure

Sentences for Dictation:
He had a seizure.
She received a receipt.
I can't conceive of the conceit.
Did you perceive the ceiling?
We enjoy the leisure time during vacation.
Neither the rain nor the snow kept us from the baseball game.

Practice Phrase: veils deceive

ch

ch₁ chin /ch/
ch₂ Christmas /k/
ch₃ Chicago /sh/

ch₃ Chicago /sh/

Words for Dictation:
machine   brochure   parachute   champagne
chute   Michigan

Practice Phrase: I ate chili at Christmas in Chicago.

The y Spelling Rule

Rule:

In words ending in **y**...

If a consonant precedes the letter y, then y changes to i before any suffix is added, except for ing and ist. The y is retained after ing and ist in order to preserve the /i/ or /e/ sound.

Examples:

spy	+ ed	= spied	happy	+ ness	= happiness	
defy	+ ing	= defying	lobby	+ ist	= lobbyist	
copy	+ ist	= copyist	conform	+ ist	= conformist	

Drill: _____

cry + ing = _____	hurry + ing = _____
rely + ance = _____	stray + ed = _____
pray + er = _____	supply + ed = _____
worry + ing = _____	healthy + er = _____
joy + ful = _____	smoky + ness = _____
enjoy + ment = _____	spy + ing = _____
say + ing = _____	funny + est = _____
sleep + less = _____	funny + er = _____
glory + ous = _____	tiny + er = _____
delay + ed = _____	injury + ous = _____
merry + est = _____	multiply + ed = _____
merry + er = _____	multiply + ing = _____
study + ing = _____	envy + ous = _____
busy + ness = _____	beauty + ful = _____
lonely + ness = _____	employ + ment = _____
pay + able = _____	

Sentences for Dictation:

This is the funniest thing I have ever seen.

The plane is flying in foggy weather.

Studying is our business.

The employer multiplied the supplies.

It is glorious to see beautiful puppies enjoying healthier lives.

Frank was crying in prayer because he was envious of his
   brother's employment.

ie-ei Spelling Rule

Rule:
Put **i** before **e** except after **c** or when it says /ā/as in neighbor or weigh.

receive	conceit	vein	believe	veil
deceive	neighbor	eight	chief	reign
receipt	weigh	sleigh	deceit	their
ceiling	reindeer	freight	heir	perceive
conceive				

Silent Letters

• **k**...	**k**now	**k**nee	knit	knob	knot
			knap	knack	knob
			knife	knock	know
			knell	known	knew
			knee	knurl	knuckle
			knave	knight	knocker

. **w**...	**w**rong	**w**rite	writing	written	wrench

. **b**...	lam**b**	com**b**	thumb	numb	whistle
			listen	castle	hasten

Comb the lamb.

Plural Endings

1. The most common way to form the plural is to add **s**.
   dog + **s** = dog**s**

2. Nouns ending in **s**, **x**, **z**, **ch**, or **sh** form the plural by adding **es** to the singular. One can hear two syllables when addding **es**.

s

miss + es = misses	bus + es = buses
dress + es = dresses	kiss + es = kisses
loss + es = losses	class + es = classes
pass + es = passes	illness + es = illnesses

x   **z**

wax + es = waxes	quiz + es = quizzes
box + es = boxes	fizz + es = fizzes
tax + es = taxes	fuzz + es = fuzzes
fox + es = foxes	
annex + es = annexes	

ch

ditch + es = ditches	stretch + es = stretches
church + es = churches	bench + es = benches
lunch + es = lunches	torch + es = torches
branch + es = branches	switch + es = switches

sh   **tch**

sash + es = sashes	slash + es = slashes
rash + es = rashes	blush + es = blushes
dash + es = dashes	brush + es = brushes
dish + es = dishes	flash + es = flashes

Irregular Plurals

mouse - mice	woman - women
ox - oxen	man - men
foot - feet	goose - geese
child - children	tooth - teeth

3. Nouns ending in **y** after a vowel form the plural by adding **s**.

boy + **s** = boy**s**

joy - joys	ploy - ploys	monkey - monkeys
ray - rays	delay - delays	donkey - donkeys
jay - jays	spray - sprays	decoy - decoys

4. Nouns ending in **y** afer a consonant form the plural by changing **y** to **i** and adding **es**.

lady changes to ladi + **es** = ladies	
fly - flies	spy - spies
ruby - rubies	pony - ponies
party - parties	lily - lilies

5. Plural of nouns ending in **o**, add **s**, if **o** follows a vowel.

studio + **s** = studios	
ratio - radios	piano - pianos
auto - autos	trio - trios

Some words ending in **o** after a consonant may spell their plural with **s** or **es**.

Exceptions:
negro - negroes	hero - heroes
no - noes	potato - potatoes
tomato - tomatoes	echo - echoes
torpedo - torpedoes	veto - vetoes

6. Most nouns ending in **f** or **u** form their plurals regularly by adding **s**.

roof + **s** = roofs		
cliff - cliffs	muff - muffs	reef - reefs

Some nouns ending in **f** or **fe** form their plurals by changing to **ve**.

leaf changes to leave + **s** = leaves		
elf - elves	wolf - wolves	life - lives
wife - wives	calf - calves	hoof - hooves
half - halves	theif - theives	knife - knives

"A teacher affects eternity. He can never tell where his influence stops."
H. B. Adams

Rule:
- A possessive is a word that tells who owns something.
- An apostrophe (') comes before an **s** to tell who owns something.

Examples:

the boy's bird	Susan's dog
a girl's bike	the children's games
a bird's nest	the teacher's apple
Mary's birthday	the plant's leaves
John's cousin	the cowboy's boots
Mother's hammer	the boy's pants
Father's apron	the book's cover
sister's fishing rod	the dog's bones
the pony's tail	the tree's apples

- In general, singular possessives add an apostrophe (**'s**).
- Plural possessives add an **s** and an apostrophe (**s'**).

Examples:
- many cats' paws
- several childrens' books
- Most hospitals' emergency departments are open all night.

Contractions

Rule:
- Contractions are words which are shortened by leaving out some letters.
- Use an apostrophe in the place where a letter or letters are omitted.

she is	she's	he will	he'll
it is	it's	you will	you'll
here is	here's	we will	we'll
there is	there's	there will	there'll
where is	where's	she will	she'll
that is	that's	I will	I'll
are not	aren't	let us	let's
did not	didn't		
does not	doesn't	I am	I'm
was not	wasn't	I will	I'll
do not	don't	I would	I'd
can not	can't		
were not	weren't	you are	you're
could not	couldn't	they are	they're
will not	won't	we are	we're
would not	wouldn't		
is not	isn't	we have	we've
has not	hasn't	I have	I've
had not	hadn't	you have	you've
have not	haven't	they have	they've

Prefixes

Rule:
A prefix is a syllable joined at the beginning of a word.

pro
for, in favor of

en
to put into or on

re
back, again

un
not

dis
not, away, apart

in
not

con
with, together

ex
out

com
with, together

de
down, away

pre
before

Note: ————————— **ad**
Some prefixes change   to, toward, for
to match the root word.
Note that these words have a
double consonant:
 e.g. ad + pear = appear.
The **d** in this prefix
changes for euphony.

pro	**en**	**re**
procedure	enclose	recall
proceed	encourage	recover
produce	enjoy	remodel
program	enlighten	remove
progress	enlist	replace
project	enroll	rearrange
prolong	endanger	refill
propose	endurable	reconsider
pronoun	entwine	reprint
protrude	engulf	refund

un	**dis**	**in**
unable	disagree	incomplete
uncertain	dishonest	inconsistent
unclear	disorder	inconvenient
uncover	disqualify	informal
uneven	disregard	inside
unaided	disappearance	inattention
unbalanced	discolor	inhuman
unpack	disobedient	insecure
untruth	dislocate	insincere

con	**ex**	**com**
concave	exact	combine
concede	examination	commission
concern	exchange	commotion
conclude	excuse	compact
conform	exempt	compartment
confuse	excavate	complaint
consent	expand	complete
consignment	extinguisher	compound
context	extraction	compress
connect		compromise

ad	**de**	**pre**
adhere	decode	prearrange
appear	deface	prebrake
accept	defeat	preheat
approach	deform	prepaid
appreciate	defrost	preschool
appetite	demerit	preview
advance	depart	prehistoric
advice	depress	preoccupied
admit	detour	prewar
appoint		
arrive		
assist		
attract		

Rule:
- A suffix is a syllable added to the end of a word making a new word.
- **ful** has only one l.
- **ly** is added to base word as it stands: safe**ly**, soft**ly**

ment state of	**y** marked by	**ful** full of	**able** possible to
agreement	airy	careful	available
astonishment	cloudy	cheerful	changeable
amusement	dusty	faithful	favorable
employment	rainy	graceful	considerable
government	sandy	helpful	profitable
	chilly		

tion state of, act of	**ance** act, fact of	**ly** like	**less** without
action	acceptance	brotherly	bottomless
adoption	acquaintance	deadly	breathless
collection	allowance	friendly	careless
direction	appearance	kindly	countless
election	attendance	kingly	needless
	inheritance	decidedly	

ous full of	**ive** that which	**al** like	**ness** state of being
dangerous	active	accidental	blindness
humorous	defective	comical	darkness
joyous	excessive	continental	gentleness
marvelous	instinctive	critical	sadness
poisonous	oppressive	medical	weakness
pompous			bitterness
prosperous			
vigorous			

ing
action going on, result of action

according
building
concerning
dealing
earning

- Words ending in **ay** or **oy** remain unchanged before any suffix...   play   playing   enjoy   enjoying

Dictionary

Oral

1. Teach the student to memorize the alphabet, if possible.

2. Break the alphabet into 4 groupings.
   abcdefg • hijkl • mnopqrs • tuvwxyz

   The idea is to divide the dictionary into quarters. We also want a student to be able to go back to the nearest beginning letter of that group. In these groupings, you have an **a** group, **h** group, **m** group, and a **t** group.

3. Lay the alphabet out on the table and have the student point to any letter you say.

adcdefg	hijkl	mnopqrs	tuvwxyz

4. Ask the student to name the letters in the h group, the t group, the m group, and the a group.

5. Name a letter and ask the student to name and point to the group in which it belongs.

6. Ask the student to close his or her eyes and point to the approximate group (in quarters) as you name a letter.

Written

1. Remove the alphabet and ask the student to write the letters of the alphabet in order.

2. If the cursive needs work, improve the writing of the letters first; then have the student place small letters in the correct order.

3. Make a ditto leaving out letters in which the student has to name and write the correct letters.

   a b __   a __ c   __ b c

Alphabetizing

1. Put some words on small cards and ask the student to put them in alphabetical order by the first letter.

2. Alphabetize the first two letters:
   money   make   must   mike   men

3. Alphabetize the first three letters:
   cat   cable   cage   cactus   camel   car

4. Alphabetize by the first four letters:
   program progress problem profile promise profit

Looking Up Words

1. Teach the student to open the dictionary 1/4 of the way for the letter **f**, 1/2 for an **m**, and 3/4 for a **t** word.

2. Teach the meaning of a **guide word**. Guide words are the two words at the top of the dictionary page. They tell the first and last words on the page.

3. Teach the meaning of an **entry word**. The entry word is the word the student is looking up..

4. Give students practice in looking up words and finding meanings and spellings.

Accent

1. Teach syllables and then teach accent.

2. Alice Koonz of the Orton Dyslexia Society teaches syllables and accent by clapping each syllable. Teach by clapping loudly and high on the accented syllable and softly and lower for the unaccented syllable.
   Example: apartment

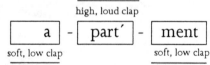

3. Use nonsense words to practice changing the stress:
   drom´ bat lam
   drom bat´ lam
   drom bat lam´

4. Teach how unaccented syllables become schwas:
   fim saf dom´
   fim saf´ dəm
   fim´ saf dəm

• Also, see pages, 47, 51, 71, 72.

Homonyms

Homonyms:
Have the same pronunciation but different meanings and spellings. These are very difficult for dyslexic students.

son	eight	mail	way	pale	for	fur
sun	ate	male	weigh	pail	four	fir
they're	to	here	hair	fair	blue	no
there	too	hear	hare	fare	blew	know
their	two					
new	see	write	wood	dear	red	our
knew	sea	right	would	deer	read	are
						hour
sent	by	mist	past	tacked	ducked	pact
cent	buy	missed	passed	tact	duct	packed
	bye					
tracked	mast	must	pair	rode	roll	teem
tract	massed	mussed	pear	road	role	team
cell	great	chord	wrap	knot	week	heel
sell	grate	cord	rap	not	weak	heal
made	so	beet	sail	dye	tale	pane
maid	sew	beat	sale	die	tail	pain
	sow					
fare	tee	prince	knows	steel	ring	daze
fair	tea	prints	nose	steal	wring	days
led	peak	bear	site	one	bough	steak
lead	peek	bare	sight	won	bow	stake
gate	reign	wait	be	meat	brake	do
gait	rain	weight	bee	meet	break	dew
	rein					

The following words have a Latin base and are connected by a vowel. They are confusing to children who have been taught to pronounce vowel combinations as a sound.

- Teach the student to divide these words into syllables.
- Teach that the i says /ē/.
- Practice dictation, spelling and reading by syllables.

i connective words /ra di o/

radio	union	Cheerios	junior
radius	onion	indio	librarian
ratio	million	opinion	radiant
billion	opium	radium	trillion
bullion	curio	stadium	stallion
magnolia	folio	auditorium	senior
familiar	portfolio	comedian	zodiac
Indian			

actual	vacuum	manual	cameo
graduate	gradual	oleo	stereo

Glossary of Terms

ADD or ADHD	Attention Deficit Disorder or Attention Deficit/Hyperactive Disorder
Blending	Moving from one sound to another to make a word, e.g. m... a... n = man. The key to blending is to "hold onto" the sounds and the word.
Consonants	All letters of the alphabet excepting vowels.
Continuous Sounds	Sounds you can say and hold for several seconds without repeating, e.g. the first sound in mat, sap, and fad. All vowels are continuous sounds.
Decode	To read by breaking apart the components of a word; blending of sounds together to make a word.
Digraph	Two letters making one sound - /sh/ /th/ /wh/ /ch/ /ph/
Diphthong	Two vowels making two separate sounds but said as one sound; e.g. *ou* in house, *oi* in oil.
Dysgraphia	Difficulty in hand writing.
Encode	To spell, using auditory sense to help put together the components of a word.
Grapheme	The written representation of a phoneme or letter sound.
Kinesthetic	Motor (handwriting).
Phoneme	Smallest unit of sound, e.g. /b/, /t/, /m/, etc.
Phoneme Segmentation	The ability to hear distinct sounds (phonemes) within a syllable. Also called **Phonological Awareness**.
Phonics	The sounds and symbols of a language.
Schwa	/ə/ a pronunciation symbol which occurs frequently in unaccented syllables in the dictionary. The sound is /u/.
Stop Sounds	Sounds that cannot be held, e.g. /p/, /t/, /g/, /j/. Do not hold stop sounds. Say sound quickly and avoid putting an uh sound after it.

Note:
/ / encloses a sound

Syllable   A word or part of a word always having a vowel sound.

car - pen - ter = 3 syllables

o - pen = 2 syllables

man = 1 syllable

The six types of syllables - summary...

closed vc/	silent v̄cȩ	open v̄/	consonant ble, dle...	"r-controlled" v"r"	vowel team cvvc
am	fame	ba	ble	or	oa
ped	ese	fe	dle	ar	oe
mop	ete	spi	fle	er	ie
cut	cute	mo	gle	ir	ee
tram	frame	cu	kle	ur	ea
fil	ile	re	tle		ou
mit	ite		zle		au
					ue
		Page Number			oi
16, 37	43	49	55	60 - 63	37

Unvoiced Sounds   Sounds made when the vocal chords do not vibrate e.g. /f/, /p/, /t/, /k/, etc. They cannot be heard from a distance but they do have an audible sound.

Voiced Sounds   Sounds made by vibrating the vocal chords, e.g. /g/ gum, /z/ zoo. All vowels, long and short, are voiced. Put your hand on your throat to feel the vibrations when the sound is made. They can be heard from a distance.

Vowels   a, e, i, o, u, y
Long vowels say their names, except for y which says /ē/ and /ī/. Short vowels are unmarked. /a/ apple, /e/ Ed, /i/ it, /o/ ox, /u/ up, and y saying /i/ gym.

Books and articles for further reading:

Adams, Marilyn Jager. *Beginning to Read*. Cambridge: MIT Press, 1991.

Alexander, A.W., Andersen, H.G., Voeller, K.K.S., & Torgesen, J. K. (1991). "Phonological Awareness Training and Remediation of Analytic Decoding Deficits in a Group of Severe Dyslexics." *Annals of Dyslexia*, 41, 193-206.

Barkley, Russell A. *Attention-Deficit Hyperactivity Disorder: A Handbook for Diagnosis and Treatment*, New York: Guilford Press, 1990.

Brown, Roger. *Words and Things*. New York: Free Press of Glencoe. Springfield, IL: Charles C. Thomas, 1983.

Bryson, Bill. *Mother Tongue: English and How it Got that Way*. New York: Avon Books, 1990.

Chall, Jean. *Learning to Read: The Great Debate*. New York: McGraw Hill, 1967.

---- *Stages of Reading Development*. New York: McGraw Hill, 1983.

Clark, D.B. (1988). *Dyslexia: Theory and Practice of Remedial Instruction*. Parkton, MD: York Press.

Duane, Drake, Rawson, Margaret: *Reading Perception and Language*. The Orton Society, 1975.

Duane, Drake and Rome, Paula D., eds. "The Dyslexic Child". New York: Insight Publishing, 1977; reprinted from *Pediatric Annals*,(8; Nov. 11 1979).

Enfield, Mary Lee and Green, Victoria. *Project Read Guides*. Bloomington, MN: Language Circle, 1988.

Gardner, Howard. *Frames of Mind*. New York: Basic Books, 1983.

Geschwind, Norman. "Why Orton was Right". *Annals of Dyslexia*, (32,1982), 13-30.

Geschwind, Norman and Galaburda, Albert M., ed. *Cerebral Dominance: The Biological Foundations.* Cambridge: Harvard University Press, 1984.

Gillingham, Anna and Stillman, Bessie. *Remedial Training for Children with Specific Disability in Reading, Spelling and Penmanship.* Cambridge: Educators Publishing Service, 1977.

Guyer, B.P., & Sabatino, D. (1989). "The Effectiveness of a Multisensory Alphabetic Phonetic Approach with College Students Who Are Learning Disabled." *Journal of Learning Disabilities,* 22 (7), 430-434.

Healy, Jane. *Endangered Minds.* Simon & Schusler. 1990.

---- *Your Child's Growing Mind.* New York: Doubleday Books, 1987.

Hutcheson, L., Selig, H., & Young, N. (1990). "A Success Story: A Large Urban District Offers a Working Model for Implementing Multisensory Teaching into the Resource and Regular Classroom." *Annals of Dyslexia,* (40), 79-96.

Levine, Melvin. *Keeping a Head in School.* Cambridge: Educators Publishing Service, 1990.

Ogden S., Hindman, S, & Turner, S.D. (1989). "MultisensoryPrograms in the Public Schools: A Brighter Future for Learning Disabled Children." *Annals of Dyslexia,* (39), 247-67.

Orton, Samuel Torrey. *Reading, Writing and Speech Problems in Children: A Presentation of Certian Types of Disorders of the Language Faculty.* W.W. Norton, 1937, paperback, 1973.

---- *Reading, Writing, and Speech Problems in Children.* New York: W.W. Norton, 1937

---- *Intimacy with Language.* Baltimore: Orton Dyslexia Society, 1987.

---- *Language and Literacy.* Baltimore: Orton Dyslexia Society,1989.

Rawson, Margaret. *Many Faces of Dyslexia*. Baltimore: Orton Dyslexia Society, 1992.

---- "Dyslexia," *Scientific American*, (256; Mar, 1987), 34-41.

Simpson, Eileen. *Reversals*. Boston: Houghton-Mifflin, 1979.

Slingerland, Beth H.. *A Multisensory Approach to Language Arts for Specific Language Disability Children*. Educators Publishing Service, 1971.

Stevens, Suzanne H. *Classroom Success for the Learning Disabled*. Winston-Salem: John F. Blair, 1984.

Stoner, J.C. (1991). "Teaching At-Risk Students to Read Using Specialized Techniques in the Regular Classroom." *Reading and Writing*, (3, 19-30).

Traub, Nina. *Recipe For Reading*. Educators Publishing Service, 1979.

Vail, Priscilla. *About Dyslexia -Unraveling the Myth*. Modern Learning Press, 1990.

Vail Priscilla. *Smart Kids with School Problems*. New York: E.P. Dutton, 1987.

Vellutino, Frank. *Dyslexia: Theory and Research*. Cambridge: MIT Press, 1979.

Wender, Paul. *The Hyperactive Child, Adolescent, and Adult*. New York: Oxford University Press, 1987.

Wilson, Barbara. *Wilson Reading System*. Hopedale, MA: Educomp, 1988.

Witelson, Sandra F. "Developmental Dyslexia: Two Right Hemispheres and None Left. " *Science*, (195; 21 Jan, 1977), 309-311.

Wren, Carol T., ed. *Language Learning Disabilities: Diagnosis and Remediation*. Rockville, MD: Aspen Systems Corp., 1983.

APPENDIX

A B C D E F

G H I J K L

M N O P 2 R

S T U V W

X Y Z

a b c d e f

g h i j k l

m n o p q r

s t u v w

x y z

Cursive Writing

I. Ovals or Roundies

a c d g o q

1 'o clock

a c d g o q

acdgoq cod dad, etc.

II. Loopies

b e f h k l

befhkl bell flee beef

bed dock flock hall etc.

III. Ups and Downs

i j p t u w (v y)

ijptuw tip pit wit

make words with all above

IV. Humpies

m n v x y z

mnvxyz

V. Odd Balls

r s sass miss rim

VI. Bridge Over's

b v w o be va wr ot

abcdefghijklmnopqrstu

klmnopqrstuvwxyz

TUTOR OBSERVATION SHEET

Student _____

Supervisor _____

Tutor _____

TEACHING OBJECTIVE	TEACHING TASK	STUDENT RESPONSE	COMMENTS
I DRILL	95% accuracy of sounds	Phonics Cards	Still confusing /sh/ and /ch/. All other sounds very firm.
II WRITING Letter Formation	Joined a,o,c,d,g and q wrote 3 letter words accurately.	Roundies words: cod, dog, cad, god	No "gaposi"s. Good! Good small muscle control.
III SPELLING	Wrote words from dictionary.	Phrases and words with ll, ff, ss, zz	Excellent instruction. He remembered the rule.
IV READING	Student read aloud with 95% accuracy.	Merrill "Dig in"	Blending coming along well but is still hard for him. Point to left of word saying "1st sound, 2nd sound" and blend by himself. He still wants to guess at unknown words from the 1st consonant. Excellent lesson.

TUTOR OBSERVATION SHEET

Supervisor _____

Tutor _____

Student _____

TEACHING OBJECTIVE	TEACHING TASK	STUDENT RESPONSE	COMMENTS

ORTON/GILLINGHAM LESSON PLAN

DATE _____   NAME _____

I. DRILL

Cards - Orally _____
_____
_____

Cards - Dictated _____
_____
_____

II. WRITING HAND

_____
_____
_____
_____

III. SPELLING DICTATION

Words _____
_____

Phrases _____
_____

Sentences _____
_____
_____

IV. READING

_____
_____
_____

COMMENTS

_____
_____
_____
_____

Phonics Wheel Template

Cut out two pieces .
Cut out window in one piece only.

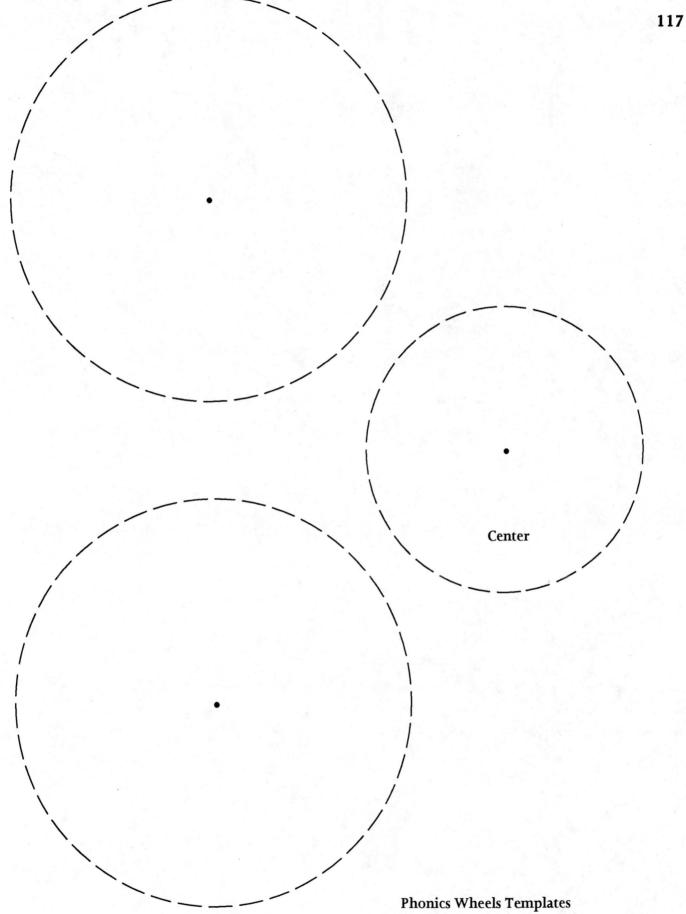

Center

Phonics Wheels Templates

A   B

BACK

FRONT

Cut out window.

Glue strip A along this edge.

Glue strip B along this edge.

Cut out notches.

| STRIPS | WORD SLIDES | BACK | FRONT |

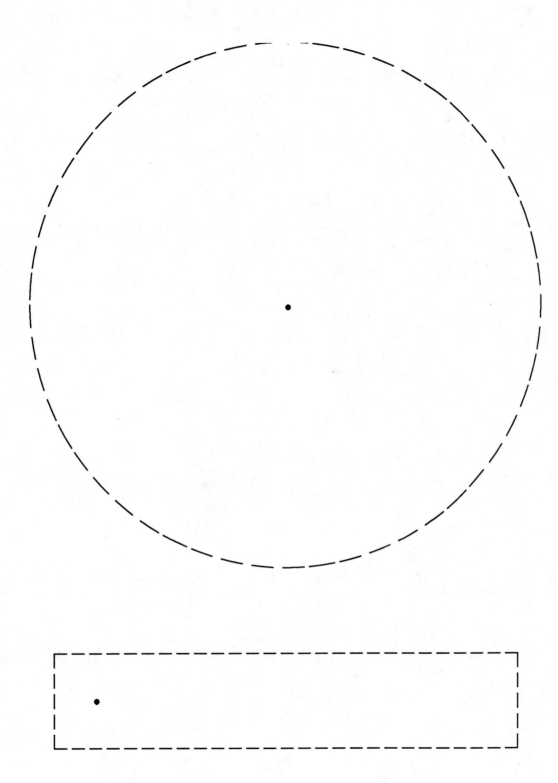

Round Word Wheel Template

ORTON-GILLINGHAM MATERIALS

BASIC EDUCATIONAL BOOKS   **OR**   EDUCATORS PUBLISHING SERVICE, INC.
420 Bell St.   75 Moulton Street
Edmonds, Washington 98020-3183   Cambridge, Massachusetts 02138-1104
• TEL 1-206-775-4710   • TEL 1-800-225-5750
• FAX 1-206-670-1737   • FAX 1-617-547-0412

Product ....Grade
Primary Phonics Strorybooks K-2
More Primary Phonics Storybooks..........................K-2
Stories From Sounds 2-3
Phonetic Primers...1-3
Recipe For Reading Storybooks K-3
Primary Phonics Workbooks...................................K-2
Explode the Code Reading/Workbooks K-4

TEACHER'S RESOURCE BOOKS
Word Attack Manual, Josephine Rudd.....................6-10
Solving Language Difficulties, Steere, Peck and Kahn...............4-6
How To Teach Spelling/How to Spell, Rudginsky-Haskell ..1-12
Spelling Workbooks, Mildred Plunkett 2-12
Writing Skills 1 and 2, Diana H. King 4-adult
Cursive Writing Skills, Diana H. King.................7-adult

---

MODERN CURRICULUM PRESS   SRA SCIENCE RESEARCH ASSOCIATES, INC.
13900 Prospect Road   P.O. Box 543
Cleveland, Ohio 44136   Blacklick, Ohio 43004-9902
• TEL 1-800-321-3106   • TEL 1-800-843-8855
• FAX 1-216-238-0460   • FAX 1-614-860-1877

Phonics Practice Readers   Grade   Merrill Linguistic Reading Program   Grade
Series A   Set 1,2,3 and 4 1-2   Levels A through F...................................K-3
Series B   Set 1,2,3 and 4 1-2
Series C   Set 1,2,3 and 4 1-2   Basic Reading Series 1-2
                                                 Readers A through F

Sound-Spelling Checklist

Student Checklist

m	a_1	s_1	f	b	i_1	h	j	k	p	t	c_1	o_1
r	l	n	g	ck	th_1	th_2	u_1	d	e_1			

ch_1	tch	sh	w	wh	v	y	z	x	qu	s_2	ph

Beg. con. Blends — **End Blends** — **Spelling ll ff ss zz**

a_2	e_2	i_2	o_2	u_2	u_3
a-e	e-e	i-e	o-e	u-e	

u-e_1	y-e	Hard and Soft C	Hard and Soft G	dge	ed_1	ed_2	ed_3	y_1	y_2	y_3

Syl. Div. Rule #1 — **Spelling Doub. Rule** — **Spelling Silent e**

Wild Old Words	Syll. Div. Rule #2	ck Spell. Gen.	ing etc.	ble etc.	Sight Words	or	ar	er	ir	ur	a_3	tion	$sion_1$	$sion_2$

ch_2	a_4	o_3	u_4	Syl. Div. Rule #3	tch Spell. Gen.	dge Spell. Gen.	oa	oe	ee	ai	ay	oi	oy	oo_1	oo_2	ow_1	ow_2	ie_1	ie_2

Spelling y Ending — **Spelling ie-ei** — **Silent Letters**

ou_1	ou_2	au	aw	ea_1	ea_2	ea_3	ey	igh	eigh	ue_1	ue_2	ew_1	ew_2	ei_1	ei_2	ch_3

Ending Plurals	Possessives	Contractions	Prefixes	Suffixes	Dictionary	Accent	Homonyms

3 Syllable Irregular

Pronunciation Key

a_1-/a/	s_1-/s/	o_1-/o/	u_1-/u/	ch_1-/ch/	ow_1-/ou/	ue_1-/ōō/	ei_1-/ā/
a_2-/ā/	s_2-/z/	o_2-/ō/	u_2-/yü/	ch_2-/k/	ow_2-/ō/	ue_2-/yü/	ei_2-/ē/
a_3-/o/ä	c_1-/k/	o_3-/ə/	u_3-/ə/	ch_3-/sh/	ou_1-/ou/	ew_1-/yü/	
a_4-/ə/	c_2-/s/	th_1-voice	u_4-/ōō/	ed_1-/ad/	ou_2-/ōō/	ew_2-/ōō/	
		th_2-unv.		ed_2-/t/	ea_1-/ē/		
				ed_3-/d/	ea_2-/e/		
				y_1-/ī/	ea_3-/ā/		
				y_2-/ē/			
				y_3-/ī/			

Additional key (center column):
- $sion_1$-/shun/
- $sion_2$-/zhun/
- oo_1-/ōō/
- oo_2-/ŏŏ/

ch_1-/ch/	ed_1-/ ad/
ch_2-/k/	ed_2-/t/
ch_3-/sh/	ed_3-/d/
u-e_1-/yü/	ie_1-/ī/
u-e_2-/ōō/	ie_2-/ī/

Writing Check List

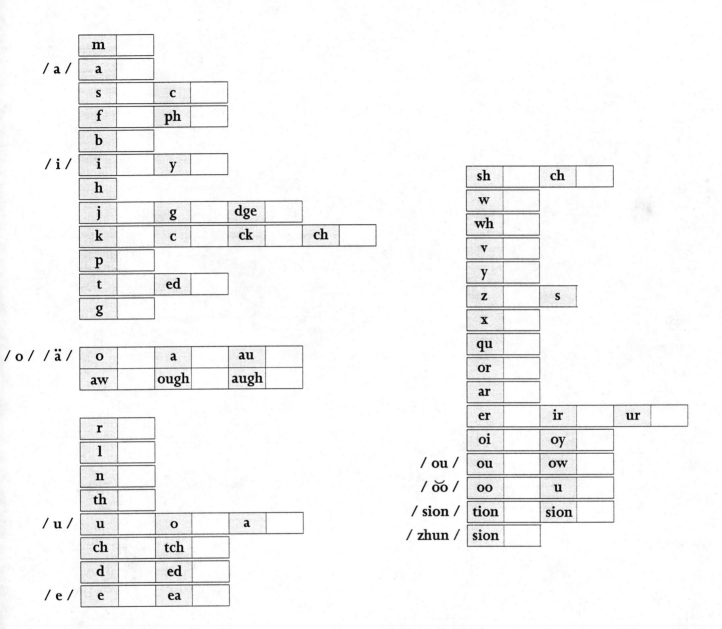

	m					
/ a /	a					
	s	c				
	f	ph				
	b					
/ i /	i	y				
	h					
	j	g	dge			
	k	c	ck	ch		
	p					
	t	ed				
	g					

/ o / / ä /	o	a	au
	aw	ough	augh

	r		
	l		
	n		
	th		
/ u /	u	o	a
	ch	tch	
	d	ed	
/ e /	e	ea	

	sh	ch
	w	
	wh	
	v	
	y	
	z	s
	x	
	qu	
	or	
	ar	
	er	ir	ur
	oi	oy
/ ou /	ou	ow
/ ŏŏ /	oo	u
/ sion /	tion	sion
/ zhun /	sion	

/ ā /	a-e	a	ai	ay	eigh	ea	ei
/ ē /	e-e	e	ee	y	ey	ea	ie	ei
/ ī /	i-e	i	igh	y	ie	y-e
/ ō /	o-e	o	oa	oe	ow
/ yü /	u-e	u	ue	ew	eu
/ o͞o /	u-e	u	ue	ew	oo	ou